A BEGINNERS JOURNEY TO THE PARANORMAL

UNDERSTANDING THE PSYCHIC EXPERIENCE

JULIA CONRAD

BALBOA.PRESS
A DIVISION OF HAY HOUSE

Balboa Press books may be ordered through booksellers or by contacting:

Balboa Press
A Division of Hay House
1663 Liberty Drive
Bloomington, IN 47403
www.balboapress.com
1 (877) 407-4847

Because of the dynamic nature of the Internet, any web addresses or links contained in this book may have changed since publication and may no longer be valid. The views expressed in this work are solely those of the author and do not necessarily reflect the views of the publisher, and the publisher hereby disclaims any responsibility for them.

The author of this book does not dispense medical advice or prescribe the use of any technique as a form of treatment for physical, emotional, or medical problems without the advice of a physician, either directly or indirectly. The intent of the author is only to offer information of a general nature to help you in your quest for emotional and spiritual well-being. In the event you use any of the information in this book for yourself, which is your constitutional right, the author and the publisher assume no responsibility for your actions.

Any people depicted in stock imagery provided by Getty Images are models, and such images are being used for illustrative purposes only. Certain stock imagery © Getty Images.

Print information available on the last page.

ISBN: 978-1-9822-5126-0 (sc)
ISBN: 978-1-9822-5128-4 (hc)
ISBN: 978-1-9822-5127-7 (e)

Library of Congress Control Number: 2020913152

Balboa Press rev. date: 07/27/2020

Do you know what you are? You are a manuscript of a divine letter.

You are a mirror reflecting a noble face. This universe is not outside of you. Look inside yourself; everything that you want, you are already that ....

~ Rumi

Dedicated to my spirit guide Emily for having to put up with me through this crazy life. And my son Branden for encouraging me through my journey of writing this bookss. I cannot forget my grandson Noah, a very special psychic child in my life.

CONTENTS

CHAPTER ONE

UNDERSTANDING PSYCHIC ABILITIES

You picked up this book, and this tells me something about you. Curiosity about psychics and their abilities has crossed your mind. Perhaps you are psychic and just haven't accepted your abilities yet, or you just are uncertain, even unaware, that what you are experiencing is in fact a psychic experience.

I absolutely get it because that is exactly what happened to me for many years. One thing I want you to know is that you are not alone. In fact, there are many of us, and we are all over the world. I personally had no idea that the things I was experiencing while growing up was in fact psychic abilities. And, like many other people, I, too, have had this preconceived notion about what being psychic is all about. I believed what was set before me by society, Hollywood movies, religion and the typical idea that all psychics have the same abilities and are ready to disclose your future full of love, a fantastic career and money in the bank.

I used to think I was anything but psychic because I don't read palms or tell people their future. Sure, I see, and experience ghosts all the time, but so does everyone if they are in the vicinity with one, don't they? That was before I realized that everyone is, in the vicinity, of one quite often, and, no, they don't always experience them, even if they are psychic.

I would like to dispel the main misunderstandings about psychic abilities. For example, we don't all have the same abilities, as you are soon to find out in this chapter. We cannot guarantee every loved one to show up every time. We are not fortune tellers. And we don't all see the future.

In fact, there are many different abilities. Each one is quite different from each other, but even if we have the same abilities, we tend to experience it slightly different from one another. There truly is no psychic normal, nor is there any specific way when receiving information. I personally have found, by working with other psychics, that we may get the same information, yet additional and different information from each other. Sometimes it can be more like, between both of us, the puzzle pieces get put together and tends to make more sense. Remember, what's coming through is often news to us too.

I would also like to clarify what to expect when you have a psychic reading done. Nothing. Expect nothing. Because in all the years I and every psychic, I have met so far, that have been doing this work realize that nothing happens the way we expect. Entering, into it with zero expectations will allow for a better reading. Also, you should know that if you show up to a reading with energy blocks it may be difficult for a psychic to get a good connection due to things like fear, anxiety, depression, preconceived notions of what will happen, doubt and any other negativity you can think of. Disappointment that it's not happening quite the way you expected. These are all reasons to cause a poor connection. If you are more interested in testing the psychic, than listening to what is coming through, you will miss so much valuable information and an opportunity for growth and understanding of your spiritual self. I recommend an energy healing before a reading if you are dealing with depression, grief or are lost in a whirlwind of negativity. Clearing that stuff out can help you relax and help the psychic get a better reading. Literally anything can come through and it's all important, even if it doesn't seem so at the moment. Trust me when I say spirit doesn't waste our time with something we are not supposed to know. If one or more of your spirit guides or Angels show up with messages, please know they have been waiting since your birth for this moment, and to disregard them, or their messages, because you supposedly don't know them, or they don't make sense, is a bigger fail than I have words to relay. Please save it for later if you don't understand it at the time. I strongly advise that you take notes or record it, because information comes through us not from us, and we often don't remember most of it, if any of it.

Psychics don't necessarily tell the future. First, of all, everyone has what is called branches, and these branches are choices that you wrote for yourself before you incarnated here. If I see only one branch and inform you of what I see, then people tend to take that branch rather than one of their other choices, or if you chose a different branch then I am dubbed as inaccurate in my reading. I personally don't tap into a client's future for this very reason. These branches are yours for the choosing. And there are ways for you to tap into your own records in order, to make your own decision based on all, of the options available. *Dr. Bruce Goldberg* has written extensively on the subject including how to access your own Akashic Records and make your own choices based on the varied potential outcome.

We don't know everything and if you have questions then please ask them. It is really, too bad when someone comes to a reading, refuses to ask questions, and has the idea that the psychic should already know what those questions are. You want answers, you need to ask questions. I have experienced spirits giving me answers before the question is asked, or before it is finished being asked, but this does not always happen. Normally, you ask the questions and the psychic receives the answers then relays it on to you. If you are afraid, they will just regurgitate the information from your questions back to you instead of an authentic answer. Then ask yourself, "Are you smart enough to know the difference?" I think you are, and then it's an invalid concern. Believe in yourself and your own ability to decipher the information that you receive.

We are only human, and we can, and do, make mistakes. Trust me when I say the guides are never wrong, but us psychics can be. We can misunderstand information coming in or misinterpret the information. In fact, studies have shown that psychics are about 80% to 90% accurate. The idea that we are either 100% accurate or

100% false is not a logical understanding of not only psychics but all humans. We are just as human as you are, please understand that.

Why are some people psychic and some are not? First, of all, everyone is psychic. When people say, "Something told me so," or, "I just had a feeling," or perhaps the word intuition rings a bell, these are all connotations for "my psychic self, told me so". But why does it seem so easy for some people to see or hear things that others cannot? My guide has told me that "psychics" have what she called a high vibratory gene, and this, is why it tends to travel in families. It's not so much that people with these genes are psychic and everyone else is not; it's that these abilities are easier to access and use for these people than it is for those who don't carry it. It only takes more work to access these abilities and that's all. I don't care who you are, do not think for one minute that someone else has a "gift" that you do not possess. I personally don't like it being called a "gift" because it gives the illusion that only special people, for whatever reason, are given this gift while the rest of the unworthy population has been left out. This is absolutely not true. Every single soul is special and equal.

Those born with this psychic gene and have easier access to these abilities may only be accessing certain abilities, not all of them, and they each experience it in slightly different ways, while in other ways it's very similar. All of it is okay because there really is no such thing as normal.

Also, everyone who is what we call psychic will have more than one ability. We never have just one. In fact, we have all of them. We just are not accessing them, so we say we are not this or that. The truth is that every human has the ability to learn how to access each one of these. Have I accessed every one of them? No, I have not, but I have access to several of them, and it is absolutely, possible that I may access more abilities in the future. And, yes, even psychics can have issues with tapping into some, if not all, of their abilities at times as well. You see, we are all different and there is no one-size-fits-all. This is so true with every other aspect of us humans, why would it not be true in this case? So, in this chapter I would like to explain and briefly discuss these different abilities in order, to create a greater understanding of what being psychic really means, and hopefully answer many questions and misunderstandings that goes along with the word psychic.

Empath - The ability to feel the emotions of others. Have you ever walked into a room of happy people and just felt the overload of happiness going on? You can't even help but be happy yourself around all that happy energy, even if you were not necessary that happy when you arrived. Your mood quickly changes. Have you ever walked into a room where everyone is unhappy, and the energy just feels heavy and dark? Even if you were in a good mood before entering this room, you immediately lose that good mood and a gloom now befalls you. This is an empath experience. On a much lighter scale of course, but you see we all have the ability, to feel energy. The difference between an empath, and the rest of the population who experiences the room energy, is that an empath feels every person's individual emotions and takes it on as their own. Example: If an empath walks by a random person in a store and neither one exchange words with each other, but the random shopper is sad for whatever reason, the empath is now sad deep within themselves as if it's their sadness. Perhaps they even need to walk outside and cry for a while and may not understand why. In fact, the deep tumultuous emotions of every shopper in the store suddenly becomes the empath's emotions. Often, I have heard people say that, "nobody knows how I feel." That is not true because the empath knows exactly how you feel. This often leads to the empath developing anxiety over public places and they often choose to become more introverted and reclusive in order, to protect themselves from the feelings of every person on the planet. Because of this, public places and social events become a source of anxiety for empaths. It has become a common place for doctors to prescribe medication for this. However, it is impossible to medicate away the abilities of the empath. I know, I've tried to do it myself and it didn't work. Coming to accept these abilities, and learning how to use them, can change this around completely for an empath. This is why I do an empath training and sharing group. This group helps to replace the medications the doctors, prescribe.

Intuitive Empath - An intuitive empath has all, of the same abilities as an empath, but they also have the ability, to see or hear things that are about to happen or that will be said minutes before it happens. This could be anything from what people are about to say or do, to an automobile accident. There are no rules stating what they may know just moments before it happens, and there is no rule stating that they will know if disaster is about to strike or that an amazing joyous event that is about to occur. It can literally be any basic, ordinary everyday stuff, as well as a life-altering experience. Before you start talking trips to Las Vegas, you should know that it doesn't happen on every occasion all day long. Yes, you can develop it to the point that it can happen more often, and by doing so, you may seem to have more "luck" than most people. My intuitive empath son who uses it to win a lot of board games may win quite often, however, he doesn't win every time.

Clairsentience - This means clear senses or clear feelings. A clairsentient has the ability, to feel into the other dimensions. They feel things stronger than other people do. For example; if a ghost is around, other people may feel as though someone, or something is near, but a clairsentient obtains a varied amount of information about the entity who is nearby. They can tell if they are male or female, child or adult, human or animal, and even personality traits and feelings. They may feel exactly where this being is standing, walking, staring and so on, yet may never actually see this ghost. They don't need to see the entity in order, to feel these things enough to obtain information about this individual. If you, or someone you know, ever felt like you are being watched or felt as though someone is in the room with you, yet see nothing, this is a clairsentient experience. The difference is that a clairsentient psychic will have these experiences quite often, quite clear and detailed, once they begin to focus on this and develop it more.

Claircognizance - Clear knowing or the ability to just know things. Have you ever just known something without being told? Nobody needed to tell you because you just knew it, but most likely you doubted yourself or brushed it off until you had some sort of proof or evidence to support your knowing. This was a claircognizant experience. A claircognizant psychic just often seems to know things and it is most often regular everyday stuff. Example: I am a claircognitive and one time I was cooking something that was turning out to have too strong of a tomato taste than it should have for what I was making. I had a knowing to add salt, and lots of it, to neutralize the tomato taste, and sure enough it fixed my recipe. Any chef probably already knew this; however, I was completely unaware of it at the time. Then I blurted out, "I don't know how I know this I just do." My son responded, "I don't know why you say that because you know exactly how you know that." He did make a very good point. I did know how I know that however, I was doubting myself and that is not okay. On the paranormal side, since that seems to be more intriguing to most people than salt, a claircognitive might go into a house with paranormal activity, or even perhaps nothing paranormal going on there, and just know events that have happened there. They don't need a vision, or to be told by the homeowner or the ghosts themselves, because they already know as if they were there when it happened. Yes, I personally have a long list of these experiences, as well as basic everyday knowing such as my salt experience and, yes, I still lose my keys often, and yes, I still have to look for them just like everyone else.

Clairaudience - Clear Hearing, now this can come in two ways, either telepathically or clear as a bell through your ear just as though you are listening to someone talk. Some psychics say it can be a higher pitch when heard from the outside. I personally hear it telepathically most of the time, however, I have heard it from the outside of my ear as well on a number of occasions. I also hear a really, loud annoying ringing in my left ear when my angels or guides wish to communicate, and I have not been communicating on a regular basis. But perhaps you could swear someone whispered your name and you turned around only to find there's nobody there. If this has happened to you, then you have had an experience with clairaudience. The difference between a clairaudient psychic and the rest of the world is that this happens to them quite often. And the communication, once developed, can be constant. If you are or have experienced this quite a bit and are unsure of it, I know it can be frightening, I assure you it is nothing to be afraid of. Once you understand it and learn to use it, you will not only become more comfortable with it, but you will be happy to use it. This is because it is quite comforting to know that you are not alone and there are people, who are in constant support of you and offering pure unconditional love for you. The person calling your name is most likely your spirit guide attempting to get your attention. Right-sided communication is negative, and the left side is positive, if it is coming from behind you it is most likely your guide, however you should still determine if it's left-sided or right-sided behind you. I cannot attest to other people and their abilities, but when communicating with earth-bound (ghosts) they project directly through my forehead. This is known as interfacing.

Clairvoyance - Clear viewing or clear sight. Have you ever closed your eyes and had a vision of someone, something, or somewhere jumps across your mind? And you did not recognize that face or wonder, what's up with that tree that just flashed before you? These visions are significant, and I recommend recording them in a journal, or whatever method it's convenient for you to do so. Have you ever seen a ghost, or thought you did? Then you have experienced clairvoyance. A clairvoyant psychic can see into the other dimensions because they get visions quite often everywhere, or almost everywhere they go. They can receive visions in waking hours, during meditation time, and pretty much anytime the visions decide to make their appearance, or an entity has decided to show up. At any given location they may see visions of the past, present or future. I remember walking through the streets of old-town Savannah, Georgia, and seeing more ghosts than people in this dimension walking around. If you only get visions of such things on occasion and this doesn't seem as prominent as I mentioned, then this doesn't necessarily mean you are not clairvoyant but perhaps your abilities are underdeveloped. And, yes, all psychic abilities even those that seem to come so easy to some people - need to be developed and worked on in order, to obtain better clarity, understanding and connecting.

Clairempathy – The ability to feel emotions of entities not currently living in our dimension. Just like the empath who feels the emotions of other people as their own, so goes for the emotions of entities not in our dimension. This is usually, but not limited, to entities that we would call ghosts. Since there are many people occupying many dimensions, all are possible.

Clairtangency - The ability to touch or feel something beyond the physical realm. I have not personally experienced this one, yet my guides have told me I have this ability, so we will just go with the generic descriptions, rather than first-hand knowledge to describe what this experience feels like, I'm told that the items feel quite solid to the psychic who has tapped into this ability. You literally reach your hand into another dimension and hold or touch an item there. Things are just as solid in other dimensions as they are here. They are simply vibrating at a different frequency.

Clairolfaction - Clear smelling, have you or someone you know ever experienced an aroma like grandma's distinct perfume after she passed? Or ever lived in house where people commonly mention smelling smoke, yet the source could never be located? Then you, or that someone you know, has experienced clairolfaction. While this psychic ability is unusual, it's defiantly not unheard of, psychics with this ability often use it to validate a loved one who passed, or to sense ghosts or spirits nearby, and can even use it to gain insight or understanding of events past, present and future. In essence; clairolfaction psychics are able to smell energy frequency in order to sense those traveling at a different frequency than our own. This unique talent is almost always accompanied by clairgustance.

Clairgustance - Clear taste, since smell and taste go hand in hand this only makes perfect sense that a clairolfaction psychic would also be clairgustance. Psychics that experience this would literally taste whatever it is that they are smelling, or even taste something they don't smell, like the taste of smoke in their mouth when there is no smoke. It could be whatever may offer a taste of something that connects them to the situation at the time. Psychics with this ability definitely can and do, learn to use it in order to better understand what they are experiencing. While it's quite typical for a psychic medium to experience clear smelling, or clear tasting, from time to time like myself, a strong clairolfaction and clairgustance psychic will experience this phenomenon quite strongly and frequently.

While this concludes the list of the clair abilities, it by no means concludes the list of psychic abilities there are out there.

Psychic Medium - What exactly is that? One misunderstanding I have noticed recently is that people suggest that psychics and mediums are two different things. I have even heard mediums themselves say this. In order, to be a medium, you must have psychic abilities to do what you do. A medium is a psychic who has learned to easily use their abilities to open, up a line of communication between them and those on the other side, be it Angels, guides, totems or loved ones. They do this by using any of the above-mentioned Clair abilities to assist in making this connection stronger. To simplify, it's like making a phone call to the other side and relaying the messages coming through the line. This could include any number of people from loved ones to Angels to guides, totems and even pets. One thing to remember if you go to a medium is that there is no control over what comes through, and anything and anyone can show up, so it is always best to arrive with zero expectations and be ready to receive anyone that does come through. They do not waste our time with stuff that you are not supposed to have or know. I know I have repeated myself here, but I would sky write it if I could.

Psychometry - The ability to "read" an object and obtain information from it through touch. This can be something small, large like a building, or even a person or animal. Absolutely everything holds energy, therefore, everything can be accessed. One can do this through touching it with a hand (preferably the left because the left one is to receive information) or put it to their forehead for the third eye to examine and look, into. This experience can be any one or more of the Clair abilities I have previously mentioned. The experience will have to do with any event that happened during the life of the object, or of a more specific energy that has attached to it. For example, an energy attached to someone's jacket and has an energy link to the person who wears it. A good example of this put into use would be if the police were looking for someone and gave a good psychometrist the jacket. This psychic could access the energy frequency of the missing person and obtain information about the person, even if the jacket was not being worn at the time of disappearance. When a psychometrist has these experiences, it may not necessarily be a major dramatic event either positive or negative.

Example: Once I touched an old cast iron skillet at a ghost town-turned tourist attraction and I saw three men sitting around a campfire just talking smiling and having a nice evening under the stars before sleeping on the ground, that night. To them this was a regular everyday experience that seemed to be no big deal, but it was a happy memory and the energy of it stayed on that pan. This is a good example as to why we should always sage items before bringing them into our home. Even new items have energy of other people on them, and antique furniture, definitely is loaded with energy. Not all negative, but because we may not know what all is attached to something, I highly recommend to sage it anyway.

Palmestry - Commonly known as palm reading and sometimes called clairology or chiromancy. I didn't include it with the Clairs because it is usually understood to be palmistry. Yes, there really are books out there that teach this, however, I don't recommend any of them. I have given myself a palm reading based on the lines of my palm and it was 100% inaccurate! Yet the best psychic reading I ever had in my life was when I was 15 years old. My cousin and I were at the county fair in New Jersey and we both decided to have our palms read. The girl doing mine was about my age and she was very good and accurate. A strong palmist doesn't need to tell you about your lifeline because they tap into the energy coming from your palm and usually tell you a little about your past, present, and future. They do this using anyone, or more, of the Clair abilities. Nothing is exact though, so remember anything can come from a psychic reading and I encourage you to go into it with no expectations to allow whatever they receive to come forward.

Telekinesis - Also known as psychokinesis, is the ability to move an object with the mind. Yes, there really are people out there who are, able to move objects with just their thoughts. I know this sounds more like a superhero or Star Wars story, but it is true. There really are telekinetic psychics out there, and truthfully, most of them are not even using their abilities, or perhaps have lost it altogether since childhood. I have a niece that is so powerful of a telekinetic that the day she came home from the hospital when she was born, she had just about everything in the house rattling. It's not uncommon for her mom to be reading her a book at bedtime and the whole bed rattles. This is untrained or undirected telekinetic abilities causing the furniture to move. And often, when going through puberty, kids will either lose this ability, or it becomes stronger and even more out of control. For example: they walk into a room and crash all of the electronics or the electricity flickers and small kitchen appliances are going off with nobody touching them, while the cabinet doors are all rattling. So many parents think they are living with a poltergeist, or some possessed house, when in fact it is their own child making it happen. At best, they are like Jedi Knights with the deliberate and controlled movement of objects. Those who manage to keep this ability into adulthood either figure out how to use it and control it, or how to suppress it in order to live what is considered a "normal" life. Suppressing any psychic ability is not healthy and it is not okay to hide it in order, to keep other people in their comfort zone. In reality this is an uneducated bubble that they want you to join them in rather than they step out of it themselves. I highly recommend T'ai-Chi for both children and adults who have this ability. There are T'ai-Chi masters who have trained themselves to move objects with the chi (energy), and they have a broad understanding as to how to use and move this energy.

Pyrokinesis - The ability to start fire with just your thoughts. Actually, this is done by using the energy around you but, yes, you must use your thoughts to accomplish this. In essence, this also is true with developed telekinesis. The movie, Carrie was based on a girl with this ability and after suffering much abuse by her mother and kids at school, and not knowing how to control it, things got out of hand when she became very emotional. The movie, of course, over - dramatized it in order to sell a lot of tickets, but essentially the idea is the same. It works similar, to telekinesis and I strongly recommend people with this unusual ability to, again, take T'ai-Chi classes in order, to know how to direct and control the

13

energy running through the body. There are many T'ai-Chi masters who have been able to control the energy around them with their thoughts and create fire out of what is seemingly thin air. However, that thin air does contain the elements that are necessary to create the fire in the first place.

Akashic Record Readings - Most people who think of a psychic think of a fortune teller informing them of what the future holds. As we have already established, this is not necessarily the case and what most psychics experience can be quite different. Psychics who do venture into the future are accessing what is called the Akashic Records and are reading directly from this source. It is a cosmic library that contains a written record of everything that ever was and ever will be. Many psychics who are able to do this don't even know this is what they are doing, they just know they see future events. If information regarding your future is what you seek, then this is the type of reading you are looking for and probably should see if the person you plan on visiting does this type of reading. But please be forewarned, only 30% of your future is fixed and you have the ability, to change and control about 70% of it. You have many opportunities to take what my guide calls branches. These branches are choices that you wrote in for yourself before you incarnated here in order to give yourself many options. When a psychic gives a future reading, they are accessing your life chart in what's called the Hall of Records. It's the library where all, of the Akashic Records are stored. This is where the famous sleeping prophet *Edgar Casey* went in order to do all of those readings, he was able to do so amazingly accurately even to this day. Yes, it is possible that they only read one branch, and you can actually take another branch but at the time of the reading they usually see what is before you based on the path you are currently on. *Dr. Bruce Goldberg* writes extensively on how to access your own Akashic Records and leave out the middleman. I'm all for teaching people to do this for themselves, rather than seeing a psychic. The reason being is that exploring your records on your own, you get to examine your many choices and decide what path you wish to take for yourself.

Telepathy - This is when a person has the ability to communicate through thoughts. They can speak and hear telepathically in their mind with humans and/or animals. Yes, the movie Dr. Doolittle is not so off course. The animals do tend to be loud from my understanding. There are many people with this ability that is just simply undeveloped, as well as many very talented people who use this quite often, I know a few myself.

Automatic writing - This is exactly how it sounds. You give your hand over to spirit and they use it to write a message. This can be done in trance, or in full consciousness, but the writing itself is automatic, rendering the owner of the hand completely out of control. Basically, the person is allowing their hand to be borrowed by spirit in order to communicate via written message. This also can be done with typing. In fact, I was asked to give my hand over and allow the Angels and my guides to write this book. Some of this book is from my own knowledge, experience, and research while some parts of this book had been written by automatic writing through spirit, as well as being directed by my Angels and guides for some of the other information. If you are interested in automatic writing yourself, I recommend just asking your Angels and guides to utilize your hand and write whatever it is they would like to communicate. Include asking questions and allowing them to write the answers. I do not recommend taking the time to write the questions down unless you write them all down beforehand and then asking them, while allowing the answers to flow. The first time I did automatic writing I scribbled a random mess all over the page, with my arm jerking in a wild manner for about fifteen minutes. So, do not be discouraged if this is how it begins, or if nothing comes in the beginning. Remember it will not come freely until you freely allow it.

Channeling - This is when a psychic step aside and allows another entity to enter their body temporarily in order to speak through them. Channeling can also be when you stay in your body, yet a spirit shares this space with you and uses your voice to speak through you. There are some very authentic and verified channelers out there, but lately it seems like there are new ones on the Internet daily waiting to share information channeled by Extra Terrestrial beings or Angels, or whomever. I advise caution when listening to unverified sources on the Internet as they can be channeling anyone from anywhere, including other channelers from anywhere or they may just be fabricating it altogether for the attention. I know some very reliable channelers and I have been present during channelings myself. I also am a channel, and I have chosen to use it for part of the information that goes into this writing, but it is not the entirety of it. When it comes to channeling, it is very important that there is proper protection in place to prevent negative-oriented entities from attempting to show up. It should never be done alone and never without an experienced channeler present. I strongly advise to err on the side of caution if this is an interest of yours. Please seek out a very experienced channeler who strongly promotes caution and questions everything. Do not take everything channeled as absolute. Positive oriented entities are happy to answer questions while the negative ones get offended quite easily when questioned. They also don't hold up very well to scrutiny. So that is one way of determining who you are dealing with.

Direct Voice - This is where a spirit uses their own voice to speak through a medium. Yes, this has happened to me. The voices can be very different from each other and not always creepy like the ones in the movies. I often get a sore throat after or even have lost my voice temporarily. This happens only when I am doing channeling work, and only when new beings I have never channeled before show up. But it never lasts long. Honestly though, I would say I prefer to use my own voice thank you. This isn't to say it is a bad thing or anything to fear, it just is another way of information coming through. If I am channeling it is never my own voice.

Teleportation - The ability to move objects from one location to another with just your thoughts. The objects disappear from one location and reappear in another location. This is extremely unusual and often found as an ability the super psychic children of China tend to possess.

Telesomatic - The ability to sense or feel someone else's emotions from a long distance away. Such as another state, or even country. This is a new one I only recently learned about as it began happening to me before I realized this is a psychic ability. I was in Arizona while my sister was in Colorado and was grieving her son, who had recently passed to the Other Side. I was continuously picking up her grief and taking it on as my own for a couple of months. Before you suggest this was shared grief, first, of all he's my nephew, not my son, and the feelings were quite different. Secondly, I had already talked to him a number, of times which made me feel much more at ease. Another thing is that because I understand so much about how our lives work and the goings on of the Other Side, I really don't grieve the way most other people do. I completely understand that there is no such thing as death and while I miss him and was sad over the fact that I was unable to help him beforehand, I really wasn't in the state my sister was in. Not even close. At first; I figured it was a combination of the fact that we are both empaths and sisters, therefore I could easily see the connection between us. This is a common and well-documented ability between twins. While we are not, twins we do share DNA and that's good enough for me. However, people with this ability, other than twins and siblings, can still connect to pretty much anyone they know regardless of where in the world they are located from each other.

Metaphysician or Psychic Surgeon - A Doctor/Healer who is capable, of making changes to the body here in the physical world through the metaphysical world. They generally have the ability, to look, into the human body and find issues that need to be healed without the use of an X-ray, ultrasound or a CAT scan. They can see inside of you. They are able, to access this issue in the astral realms and make, adjustments as well as often see what you are doing, or not doing, to create the issue. And, yes, you are doing or not doing something to create almost every sickness, ailment, disease and medical problems known to man. The first, and most important step, to healing is to accept responsibility for what you need to change Second is to absolutely want to be healed. Nothing can really be done for people who wish to stay sick. Before you say, "Who wants to stay sick?" I say you would be surprised how common it really is. I personally have seen miracles happen from a talented metaphysician. They work similar, to the average energy healer except they are capable, of taking it into an entirely new level with the ability to see into and understand the human body.

Precognition - The ability to predict future events. This can be done both in waking hours or during sleeping hours. And it could be a few minutes into the future or years. There is no guidelines as to how it is supposed to happen.

Thoughtography- The ability to burn one's own thoughts onto paper, like a photograph but without the camera.

Remote viewing - The ability to see things from a great distance. The governments of the world have been using remote viewers as spies since the Cold War.

Aura Reading - The ability to see auras. First, of all, everything has an aura around it. That means every person, rock, plant, animal, even planets have their own auras. These are the colors that are in your energy field around you. Auras have a variety of colors, and these colors do have different meanings and they do change colors from day-to-day or week-to-week, depending on what is going on with the individual at the, moment. Yet, most people will have one or two main colors that tend to stay with them always. Sometimes dominant and sometimes just as an outline, but your main colors should be present. Yes, you can and often do have more than one color surrounding you. Some psychics can see, or sense, these colors either occasionally or constantly, and absolutely your pets can see auras as well. Auras can tell a lot about a person, their personality and what they are currently experiencing. Some psychics can obtain information about past, present and future through your aura energy. The Kirilian camera can also be used to photograph the aura as well. Here's a breakdown of the aura colors and their meanings.

Red - Pertains to the heart and blood circulation.

Varied shades of red - Deep red, strong willed, grounded and realistic behaviors - Muddy Red, anger and frustration - Clear Red - passionate and energetic - Orange Red, confident and determined - Bright Pink, sensitive and compassionate - Muddy Pink, dishonest and immature.

Orange - Good Health, creative and social

Shades of orange - Orange Yellow, intelligent and detail oriented - Brownish Orange, low ambition and repressed emotions.

Yellow - Spleen, life energy, easy going

Varied shades of Yellow - Pale yellow, psychic, spiritual awareness and positivity - Bright Yellow, power struggles and controlling personality - Metallic Gold, spiritually activated and inspirational - Dark Muddy Yellow, fatigue and stress.

Green - Heart and lungs, healthy love of children, animals and nature.

Varied shades of Green - Emerald green, healer and loving person - Yellow Green, open communicator and open hearted - Muddy Green, jealousy, victim, blaming and insecurity.

Turquoise - Immune System, sensitive and compassionate.

Blue - Throat and thyroid, calm, collected, sensitive and intuitive.

Varied shades of Blue - Light Blue, Peaceful and honest - Royal Blue, Spiritual and generous - Muddy Blue, fear of expressing one's self and speaking your own truth.

Indigo - Pituitary Gland, deep emotions, intuition and sensitivity.

Violet - Pineal Gland, nervous system, intuitive, visionary and psychic abilities.

Lavender Imagination, creator and dreamer.

Silver - Strong and powerful color used for binding. It connects us all together including people, animals, nature, the cosmos and the other side. Dirty Grey - blocking energy flow

Gold - Divine protection, guidance and wisdom.

Black - Unforgiving nature, anger, grief, health issues and depression.

White - Healthy, truthful, pure intensions.

Brown - Greedy, self, absorbed and closed minded. Also; could be related to depression.

Other psychic terms that should sound familiar to you, and that everyone has and will experience sometime in their lifetime, is precognition, knowing something just before it happens. Intuition translates into protective sight. "Follow your intuition." Sound familiar? How about insight (seeing intuitively)? The sixth sense; does this mean we all have five senses and only psychics have a sixth sense? Or do we all have six senses and the sixth one being your intuition? I'm feeling extremely confident in saying that everyone has six senses, and it is just a matter of tuning in to all of them. L et's not forget E.S.P (extra sensory perception) which, is basically all, of our extra sensory skills that were covered in the list of Clair abilities. This is just another form of terminology for anyone of those. Don't we all have some abilities if we pay attention to them? Absolutely, we all do! Therefore, we are all psychic beings. Some abilities come easier and more natural for some people, while others have, to work at it and put in more effort. But that's okay because even some of the most powerful psychics out there have had to put in some sort of effort and work at some point in their lives. Don't you dare believe that being psychic is only for those who are special enough to receive an incredible gift and that it's not available to everyone. We are all equally special and being psychic is available to all those willing to work hard at developing the abilities that are simply lying dormant inside of them. That includes you.

CHAPTER TWO

UNDERSTANDING OUR PSYCHIC CHILDREN

Psychic children, Indigos, Crystals, Rainbow and Star Seeds! What does it all mean, and could my child be one of them? Or, even more wild, could I be one of them? These are questions you may be asking yourself. The truth is there's quite a bit to know and understand with our children, and my goal in this chapter is to bring some basic understanding of these kids to the adults who love them.

What does all of this mean anyway and what makes one child different, or more special, than another? The truth is that it means a lot and they are all different, yet the same, at the same time. Before you start thinking that you want your child to be one of these "special" children, I want you to know without a doubt in your mind that if you have a child, your child is special. Each, and every soul comes from a spark of light, created by the same source and the love of that source is insurmountable.

I really want to make something clear. The labels I will be using to refer to certain groups or types of kids, are not my labels and I will only be using them because we humans have created them, and we tend to find some level of understanding by using them. My guides have railed me to no end about the problems with using labels on these advanced souls more times than I can count. And what a disservice we are doing to our children by using them. For the sake of understanding only, I am going to be using labels.

If you happen to be a parent of one of these unique children, I strongly advise to please use discernment regarding when or how, or even if, you choose to use any of these labels when referencing your child. Labels often supports the idea that one child is more special, or better than another, and this is absolutely, farthest from the truth as we can get. It makes these "special" kids begin to think that they deserve special privileges or deserve something better than another person for being so "special," while another is not. This is a very cruel thing to teach a child. Whether deliberate or not. It's not okay to feed ego into a child and allow them to believe that they are different or separate from the rest.

Each child has a uniqueness unto themselves that should be cherished, loved, nurtured, raised and educated according to their individual needs in order, for optimum opportunities for a successful and happy life. And these kids, like all children are here to teach us, not the other way around, if only the adults would just listen. For example; when children speak of past lives they lived or just the lifetime before this one, please whatever you do, don't tell your child that this is "not true," or "stop talking like that," or "we are the only parents you have ever had." This is damaging to your child in order to stay in your own comfort zone, and that's not okay. It also teaches kids to become liars, because they might begin to lie about their experiences in order to keep the adults in their life comfortable. Why would a three-year-old make up memories of a past lifetime? Be logical here when you ask yourself this question. This is an opportunity to learn something amazing about your child and who they really are, not who you decide they are.

I have no idea how many times people have asked me if their child is an old soul because he or she keeps mentioning other lifetimes. The answer to that question is a resounding yes! Currently, every human child on this planet is an old soul. You see, we are coming to the end of a cycle, which means very difficult times. Only advanced/old souls can be here right now, and even those advanced souls, struggle to be here. A new or young soul, if you wish to look at them that way, would not be able to survive at this juncture in our earth's life cycle, therefore only the most advanced souls are incarnating right now. I mean look at the teen suicide rate! It truly is a difficult time to be here, and one of the many things that can be done in order to help your child through it is to be open and willing to listen to them.

You see, souls have been around for much longer than what we consider to be time, and all of the children have lived many lifetimes. To expect them to suppress these memories of theirs, or imply they are not telling the truth, we teach the children to be untruthful to themselves and hide who they really are. When adults tell them, these experiences are not real, and make negative comments in regard to them mentioning past lives or psychic experiences, we are damaging these children in order to not have to address something we find difficult. Instead of a negative reaction, try just listening to what they have to say. Don't pry too much, because they often tend to shut down when this happens, but please just listen or ask questions in a casual yet inquisitive way. Let them feel like you care about what they have to say. I suggest you take notes or write it in a journal, right after the fact so you don't forget what was said. And please, don't be all creepy about a journal or notes every time something comes up. It may scare them off from telling you. Keep it casual and act like it is everyday stuff. These notes will not only help you to learn so much more about who your child is, but about who you are, as well as the rest of us, and possibly get some hints of how the whole cycle really works. If you tend to make a big deal about it, or act scared, or make a negative comment, this could cause these children to feel insecure about speaking to you, or anyone for that matter when these things come up. That is really not how you create a healthy relationship with your child. Your child's sense of security should be the most important thing on your list of priorities, even if it means that you must face subject matter that you are uncomfortable with.

Children are the most psychic people on the planet and the amount of knowledge we can obtain from them is unlimited. I have met many adult psychics who are only just now learning to reconnect with their psychic self, due to the fact, that they had to repress it in order to save the parent from their own feelings they were afraid to deal with. This has caused emotional damage as well as identity struggles, anxiety and depression. Only now as adults, are they dealing with it and learning about how to allow themselves to be who they really are, and that is an amazingly beautiful soul with the ability to talk to Angels! And no surprise, some of them are raising psychic children.

I would like to briefly mention here that psychic children living in abusive and dysfunctional homes will hide or suppress their abilities, making the reconnection process later in life a part of the healing process. Suppressed psychic abilities, will continue to pop up on their own until it is acknowledged and the person hiding it begins to accept and use it. There is no true running from it throughout life and so goes with childhood traumas. Until both are acknowledged and dealt with, it will continue to pop up. Yes, it can be an extremely emotional battle, not to mention very lonely, if there are no other psychics in your circle of friends who understand this. However, this battle can be conquered, and I am living proof that suppressed childhood trauma and suppressed psychic abilities can be healed. Let's keep the next generation from having to go through this level of healing. We are responsible for helping this generation of kids to not go through what we did in order, to be who we are.

Let's move on and talk about imaginary friends. This is a very important subject that I wish all parents understood. Children do not make up imaginary friends. These entities they are telling you about are very real, and it is finally time for us to understand and acknowledge this. And again, it's very damaging to tell your child they are not real, for the same reasons already listed.

When talking about imaginary friends, before you freak out that little Bobby is conversing with demons, let's look deeper and more practically into this subject. When I say entities, I'm referring to real live living beings that just happen to be vibrating, at a different frequency than our own. That includes both negatively and positively oriented people/entities. Imaginary friends can be a wide variety of individuals whom we often misinterpret as fake, evil, or the general household pet ghost, when in reality; there's so much more to this in many of these cases. It could be one of many spirit guides here to assist your child during this incarnation. Perhaps it is one of their Angels. It could be a loved one that passed away, including ones that passed away before the child was born. My mother, who passed away before my grandson was born, was often heard talking to him on his baby monitor, as well as my daughter in law seeing her in his bedroom once. It could be a sibling that hasn't been born yet, or from another lifetime. Perhaps there really is a ghost in your house who is communicating with your child. Children are more open and psychic than most adults, therefore it is common for ghosts to contact them.

Why are the children so much more psychic than we are? First, they are newly here from the Other Side making them automatically more open than we are. Secondly, adults have more years of being told that it's not real, that it's something bad, or we should just fear it without any logical explanation other than you have no idea if they are good or bad. All of that is hogwash, yet, it seems to be so deeply engrained into the human psyche that we tend to not stop and question the logicality of it all. Children, on the other hand, have yet to adopt all this unfounded belief system we all seem to have that creates a blockage between us and them, children have no blockages to clear out.

Yes, it is possible for an imaginary friend to be something, or someone negative. But, please don't jump to that negative conclusion immediately. Children who are strong psychics, or very advanced souls, easily attract ghosts and, yes, that can include lower level entities. This is because they know they can communicate with your child. These children are like a beacon attracting everyone in town. So, what can we do to help our children with imaginary friends? First of all, don't freak out or act scared. Children can smell fear like a horse and then their fight or flight instinct immediately kicks in. They know without a doubt, they know. If you can't help but feel this way, then take a deep breath and become a pro at hiding it while you work on conquering it. Believe me, fear does nothing productive for you or your child and never has helped the situation on any level. Secondly, treat the situation like you would any other friend. If little Jenny tells you she has a new friend that moved in next door, the first thing you do is ask her about this new friend, go meet her and her parents, then most likely arrange play time in order, to better get to know each other. The key here is to get to know each other. Same with imaginary friends. Know who your kids are playing with, be interested, ask questions in a casual but interested manner. Have tea parties with her and her new imaginary friend. Ask questions of this friend, such as who are you? Where did you come from? Where do you live? How did you meet Jenny? What is your name? What are your likes, dislikes, are you an adult, or child and so on, make it very casual and mundane, Jenny will most likely tell you what the friend is saying in response, Guides and Angels sometimes show up in the form of a child in order, for the children to make a better connection with them, and feel more comfortable with them visiting.

Perhaps their imaginary friend is grandma who passed away and uses her first name when visiting. I have a friend whose son often played with an imaginary friend for a few years that he insisted was his baby brother. When his mother became pregnant again, the boy began saying he can't play with his brother now because he's in mommy's tummy. And, yep, you guessed it, she had a baby boy. Continue to ask questions and use discernment. You will easily, in time, be able to determine who it is your child visits with.

I'm not attempting to frighten anyone because that is absolutely not what this is about, and fear will never help anyone advance forward. However, we do need to address the possibility that your child's friend is a negative entity. Only through knowledge and understanding can we protect our children and that is the ultimate goal here. They are not as deceiving or as powerful as they would like you to believe. The simple questions I have already listed will flush out a negative someone in short order. Maybe not on day one, but shortly afterward. If Your child says things like, "he doesn't like you." or "he tells me to do things I am not supposed to do," or if things are broken, and the child blames the friend.

I'm not talking about just trying to get out of trouble, because my grandson blames the dog for a great many things, and even blamed his horse for spilling water on the driver's seat of my car. I'm talking about strange things that are out of character for your child. Trust yourself and use your discernment. Believe me, they do think it's quite funny to make a mess and watch your child get in trouble for it. If these things happen, I promise you no positive entity would tell your child to say or do negative things. And if this is happening, it is very important to not frighten your child. Do whatever your child needs to feel safe. If that means sleep in your room, if they feel the need to do so, or keep a light on. Whatever it is, please do it. If a neighbor kid had a habit of telling your kid to do something they are not supposed to do, you would instruct your child to stick to what they know is right and say, "Hey, I'm not going to do that," or "No I refuse to listen to you." Say it with firmness and confidence! Let them know they are in control. This is important to give them control. And you take yours as well. If little Jenny's friend was dumping flour in your kitchen and watching Jenny get busted for it, I think you would not allow that friend to come over anymore. Yes, you do have the power and ability to set your rules and boundaries. Don't use fear, but confidence, in saying things like, "No, go away. You are not welcome here!" I cannot express enough the importance of firmness and assertion at this point. Make sure your child understands that they do not need to listen to negative things from anyone, and that includes human, or ghost, or whomever.

Give them confidence and power. And, above all make sure your child knows it is okay and safe to tell you when this "friend" is saying or doing things that are not okay. And remember that your fear creates a problem, it does not solve one. I understand it is difficult to conquer, but it is necessary. That is just the first step for getting a handle on the situation. Since I will be discussing negative entities in my chapter on ghosts, I will not go into more detail here but if you feel it necessary please seek professional help with this situation. I don't mean ghost hunting groups either, but an actual psychic who can handle this kind of work. Not all of them do, therefore you really must ask before you spend the money. Explain what it is you are needing and ask if they can help or refer you to someone who can help. And not just sage the house and leave, but that they actually have the capacity to get rid of said entity.

On to monsters in the closet or under the bed. If your child tells you there are monsters in the closet or under the bed, for the love of creation, don't tell them they are not there! Just don't do it! If your child is telling you they see monsters in these locations, or anywhere else for that matter, it's because they really are there, and you are the only one they must go to and ask for protection. I cannot even begin to tell you how heartbreaking it is to know there are creepy things running around a child's room and when they ask for help, they are turned down. The fear they have is real and they really do require, some support. Do not leave a small child, or any child for that matter, to deal with it on their own. Recently my grandson informed me, as we were all sitting in the living room, that there were two monsters outside of our house. I looked out front and, sure enough, a tall dark shadow figure was standing on the curb in front of my house seemingly lost and confused as to how he got there. With some Angel help, I was able to send him back to source where he belongs in order to be reabsorbed and healed through the love of creation. I looked out back and I believe I know where the second entity had been, yet I didn't find one. However, once they know I'm coming they tend to run off and hide somewhere. If I cannot find them, I am unable to do anything about them, I just put a different barrier around my house than I currently had because he was awful close, and I don't want anything negative that close to my house. Then I reassured my grandson that Grandma took care of the monsters and he was safe. Often, he likes to sleep with the dog to help him feel safe from negative entities, and that is okay too. Animals are very psychic and protective, which is why I often recommend a dog or cat in the room to help them feel safe.

Unless your child saw a movie, read a book or was told something that gave them this idea or scared them into thinking such a thing is real, then logic dictates that they would not make up such a story. Your job as the protective parent is to evict said monster, or get someone to do it for you, but please make your child's safety and security much more important than any uncomfortable feelings that you or anyone else has regarding the situation.

For some psychic children this goes beyond past life memories and imaginary friends. For most children, these things fade between the ages of five and seven because that is when they seem to completely forget where they came from and ground themselves more into this earthly environment, as well as blocking things out and believing what they see is not real. They stop being so psychic you might say. This; is why most past life memory stories come from kids ages three to five years old because they finally have the vocabulary to talk about it while still retaining the memories. After that, they tend to forget whatever memories remained and connections to the Other Side. But the psychic children that keep this connection will begin to develop any one of the abilities listed in Chapter One. Many psychic children have struggles with the fact, that they are never alone. The truth is none of us are ever alone. And while most people are unaware of that fact these kids are fully aware of it and struggle to relay it to those who seem completely oblivious to what is really going on around them. Often, these children feel as if they are not "normal" like everyone else. While other people are unable to see, hear or feel things such as they do, they sink into an ever; deepening level of separation. Often, these children prefer to be alone rather than expose themselves to a multitude of information that bombards them when playing with other children, or even when around adults or any large crowd. They have not yet learned how to filter these things out or put up protective barriers to buffer at least some of it.

When these children feel so different and alone, they often will isolate and withdraw within themselves, not sharing with others what they are truly experiencing. Feeling as though they are the only ones in the world who feel this way. This can lead to depression, and a profound feeling of loneliness. They don't generally understand that they are simply seeing into other dimensions of reality that really does exist on levels that are just difficult for others to see or access. Yes, it may even seem as though comprehension may be out of reach for them, but I don't necessarily think so. I think it very well may be within reach for them, with proper understanding and connection within the self.

These abilities can feel heavy and burdensome. The weight of the world becomes heavier as they approach their teen years. Unfortunately, there are times when it is dealt with through rebellious behavior, drugs, alcohol, and other negative patterns. This is all due to their poor attempts at subduing these experiences and trying to dull their sensitivities to it. This can easily be noticed in their disturbing art creations or the desire to blacken up their wardrobe, and their room decor. As they lean more and more towards dark energies, they begin self-destructive behaviors and can even become suicidal.

Psychic abilities can be very overwhelming, but the good news is that there are ways to help these kids. The earlier the parents get on board with it, the better. What these children need more than anything is for someone to validate them. Tell them that they are not insane, crazy or telling lies. They desperately need someone to believe them and to know that they are not alone, and yes, there are many other people who experience this as well. Please, if you cannot talk to your child about what they are going through, or they refuse to communicate it, find someone who they can talk to who understands these experiences and how to deal with them, and help them to feel not so alone in this. There are psychic therapists and healers out there that can help if you or your child happens to need one.

Strongly encourage your child to journal and/or draw what they are experiencing. If for some reason they are unable to get it out, or to share with you, or anyone else regardless of how hard you work to give them comfort and support, give them a diary with a lock and key and let them know that it's a safe place and that nobody, including yourself will intrude in that privacy. It is important to keep that agreement, because trust is important and should be cherished on both sides.

These children often connect well with animals. Having a pet for them will do wonders. If you are unable to have a pet then look for a situation where they can be connected with animals, such as horseback riding lessons, or volunteering with an animal rescue, or regularly visit a farm or friends with pets. As much animal exposure as possible will do amazing work. I have a niece whose daughter is very psychic and enjoys spending a lot of time sitting with her dog, or her horse, all alone. I told my niece not to worry, and that this is healthy for her. I myself spent countless hours sitting with my horse, even laying down on her like a bed and just staying there for hours like that while she munched hay.

These kids require alone time, don't force them into attending social events if they really don't want to go. Finding peers with similar abilities also may help them get through the difficult teen years. A good mentor is vital to help your child learn how to filter and use these abilities to their advantage to turn what seems to be a negative into something very positive. But most importantly, this person is to help them eliminate the feelings of fear and seclusion. This can include the parent's fears and concerns.

I also strongly recommend getting your child into yoga, T'ai-Chi, Qigong or Lujong. This is something you can do together. It will teach the entire family how to move energy. Which is more important than I have the words to relay, as well as creating family bonding time when participating together. Also, take some mindful meditation classes together. This will help the entire family learn to release stress, have better open communication, and clear negative patterns.

Children require a very strong support system, so please create one. The things I have mentioned are not one or the other, but all of it combined to create a healthy environment for them to thrive in. And, above all remember that it is 100% okay for your child to be psychic and they need to know this. And whatever you do, if your psychic child is cross eyed please do not allow this to be fixed in order, to fit them into a social box, unless it really is affecting their vision. The shamans are born cross eyed and they can see into many dimensions. They become shamans through experience, which means this child has accumulated an amazing amount of experience as an advanced spiritual soul before arriving here. My grandson is slightly cross eyed and he's very psychic. They are to be respected, not fixed.

When a psychic child is nurtured and supported in their abilities, they grow into healthy confident psychic adults using their abilities to do amazing and positive things. The opposite is an emotionally suppressed individual who constantly bears the burdens of both realities and feel they must bear it alone while fighting off depression and darkness, which ultimately manifests itself into many other physical problems. Love, encouragement, and support is the key to offering these kids a balanced life full of self, love and acceptance of themselves and others, including the opportunity to be successful and well-rounded despite the challenges that come with being psychic.

I want to get into a group of advanced souls who have been, and are still, coming here in order to help all of us advance into a golden age of human change. These kids all began arriving right after the Second World War and have been incarnating in larger numbers with each group of them. I'm referring to the Indigo, Crystalline, Rainbow and the soon to be Dragonfly kids. We also have what people refer to as the Star Kids or Star Seeds.

Since this is only a chapter and not a book on these kids, I'm going to have to make a very short description of them, please note that by no means can I do them all justice with only a chapter. These children are often born with Autism, Down Syndrome, or even severe disabilities rendering them unable to walk, talk or communicate in any fashion that we understand. These kids bring an entirely new understanding to the word challenging. These kids are all too often medicated for ADHD (attention deficit hyperactive disorder) or ADD (attention deficit disorder). They often struggle with a difficult childhood due to the desire of social standards wanting all too often to stuff them into a square box when they fit into a hexagon. This just doesn't work for them, nor should it be expected to. They often need to be educated and challenged in ways that our current school system is not structured or prepared to do. They are highly intelligent and often get bored or frustrated with the way they are expected to learn. It is high time we take a good look at our educational system and why it is so broken. My daughter went all through school being told she had a learning disability and I bought it hook line and sinker. She graduated from college with honors at the top of her class. If you tell her something, or show her something she never forgets it, yet, she has always struggled to take tests or relay information read from a book. All the while, my son was always struggling in school, even though he has a photographic memory and never needed to study anything to ace a test. He simply was bored, and they refused to challenge him and teach him at his own level. Instead, they wanted me (which I adamantly refused to do) to drug him into submission and accept his fate with the public-school system. This was to include twelve years of his life being bored into a dumbfounded mindlessness and dubbed educated when he got his diploma. Children learn in many ways and that doesn't mean a learning disability. It means the child needs to learn in the capacity that suits their way of learning. These advanced children are hopefully teaching us to make these changes through their own struggles with this distorted idea of learning. And, for the love of creation, I hope that includes getting our children off the narcotics.

After a question and answer session with my guides in regard to these children, and when they began arriving, and when each group stopped arriving, they gave me the following information in regards to these beautiful souls who have come here during this incredible time on our planet. They informed me that there were four groups, and the fourth group has not begun to arrive yet. There are four groups of kids with three waves in each group. *Deloris Cannon* refers to them as the "waves of volunteers." If you are not familiar with her work, I highly recommend it.

The first group of children have been labeled as the Indigo kids. First, by *Nancy Ann Tappe* due to the Indigo color that can be seen in the Aura field around their body. This was further studied and written about by both *Lee Carroll,* and *Jan Tober.* Together their studies have led to multiple books followed by many more very experienced and qualified individuals who have written to great extent in regard to these kids. What I have gathered from my guides is that the first wave of Indigo children arrived from 1947 to 1962. The second wave of children began to trickle in as early as 1958 with the bulk of them arriving between 1968-1988, while the last of them slowing down and only finishing their arrival by 1991. The third wave began to arrive in 1988 through 2007, with the last of them only trickling in between 2005 and 2007. The Indigo children are considered the warrior group. They came to break up the dark energies that the people of earth were living in. They had to break up these dark energies to make way for the advanced children we are seeing today. There is no way these later kids could arrive, let alone survive here, the way things were. Look at the turmoil of the 60's and 70's. What did that first wave do when they arrived? They began to question everything about the way things were run, the government, schools, religion, as well as, social standards. They took to the streets, university campuses and the lawns of government buildings with the hippie peace movement with their "make love not war" slogan. This movement spanned across many continents, cultures, and languages.

These first souls had a very difficult time adjusting to this dimension, leading many of them to completely reject society altogether and start their own societies called communes, or choosing isolation and rejecting the company of others all together. This isn't because it was them who were unable to function, it was because they could clearly see and understand that the entire way of society wasn't really functioning right. The second wave of the Indigo warriors found it much easier to question things such as government, schools, authority, and religion, as well as what is accepted as old society norms. Many of these kids have no regard for authority, they often have no concern whether they get into trouble. They are highly intelligent and often don't do well in school because our school system is not designed to challenge kids that are capable of learning multiple subjects at once, or perhaps they need to learn certain subjects a grade or two ahead while remaining in their current grade for other subjects. These children often not only thrive in such challenging situations, but need such situations presented to them. For these children it is a great struggle to fit into what we have dubbed as "normal." and all too often are medicated in place of educated.

These children are often born into very abusive and dysfunctional families causing their situation to be even more difficult than it already is. I questioned my guides as to why this is, and they informed me that they were sent to break up the negative energies and stop the cycle of abuse. As my son put it they really are the warriors because they said, "Hey, I will go down there and take the beatings so someone else doesn't have to, and I am going to learn from it and refuse to continue it through the family." This is often true! The many generations of abuse stop with them! In many cases they are successful in bringing awareness and education to this problem and in many cases, they get "lost" in it causing mental instability, substance abuse and even suicide at times.

My guides said they underestimated the difficulties of this task, and while some do accomplish this task, others either become part of the negativity or incapable of completing their contract here, opt to take an early exit either scheduled or unscheduled. I personally have seen this firsthand, therefore their explanation made perfect sense. If you have or know someone who has an Indigo child or a child with Indigo traits to include the Crystals there are many good books out there to include, *"Empowering Your Indigo Child,"* by *Wayne and Ellen Dosick.*

As the third group of Indigo children arrived their numbers began to dwindle significantly in order to make way for the next group of children known as the Crystalline or Crystal children. The first of these Crystal children began to arrive as early as 1988, however, the main group of them began to appear in 1990 with the bulk of them hitting peak in 1995 and 1996. With the first wave of Crystal kids slowing down in 1997. This first group of kids often share traits of both Indigo and Crystal children. Therefore, they are often referred to as the transitional kids. They have so many pale colors in their auric field that they may look to have more of a white field around them. This group is so advanced that it is very difficult for them to incarnate here as healthy children. Some of them may never learn to walk, talk or even provide basic self-care, yet they are extremely telepathic and often have extraordinary psychic abilities. While the healthy children from this group often love music, even learning to sing before they can speak at times. These kids are psychic, have a very forgiving nature and are sensitive. They tend to love animals and nature. It is very important that the energy around them remain calm and loving as much as possible. Often, they are protege's capable of mastering several languages at a young age, or advanced math, or can play any musical instrument with an incredible amount of talent yet never took music lessons. My nephew, Kyle, was a beautiful Crystal child who was a music protege'. By age three he was playing the piano and by age six he was able to not only play music he never heard before but was able to master difficult pieces that even experienced musicians had difficulties getting just right. He could pick up any instrument and master it within a few hours without a single music lesson. Music was in him because he was a child of the universe, and the universe was created by music.

It is also commonly mentioned how these children, when born, come into this world with their eyes wide open as if they already bring a knowing with them. Those present upon their arrival also comment on such things as feeling an overwhelming peace or joy. When these children arrived the earth-energy was not yet ready for them causing much difficulties for both the healthy ones and the disabled.

The second group of Crystals began to arrive in 1996-1997 and continued their arrival at a fast pace until 2000. However, as the second group began to arrive the Earth energy was still not ready for them and so many of them still had to come in with disabilities. This seems to be the pattern all the way up to the present children. The upside to all of this is that these kids began to bring awareness to these issues like autism, as well as teaching their caregivers how to truly open-up their heart chakra and love unconditionally. They are here for us all to wake up and say, "Hey, perhaps all this processed junk food, too many vaccines before our kids have a chance to build an immune system, and the bombardment of electronics on a sensitive developing fetus is something we all need to take a look at." This is causing people to question why is it that our babies can't come into this world healthy?

As a group, these kids are beginning to challenge the ideas and understanding of the adults around them. Perhaps because it is time for the people of the Earth to wake up to their own spirituality as they look into the eyes of these kids who can teach us what it really means to be spiritual in its truest and most honest form and see what amazing souls these highly advanced and highly psychic children are. They may have physical issues in most cases, but they are not the ones with the disability. We are. And I think many people are beginning to see and understand this.

The third wave of Crystal children began to arrive around 2001 and are still arriving at the time of this writing. However, I am told they have slowed down to a trickle and will soon finish. While many of these children are still arriving with disabilities, we are seeing more and more healthy Crystal kids being born with that bright awakened look in their eyes and are ready to help change the world. Most of these children are being born to Indigo parents which I find to be no surprise, as it only makes sense to do so in my mind anyway. Advanced children need advanced parents who already came to break up the energy and prepare a better environment for them to grow up in. If you are interested in more information on these children there are many good writings about them, including, *"The Children of Now" by Meg Blackburn Losey.*

The third group of advanced children are known as the Rainbow kids. The color fields between the Crystal and the Rainbow children are only slightly different as is their level of evolvement. Basically, they are one and the same at this point. The first wave of Rainbow children began to arrive in the year 2000 and reached their peak by 2005 while tapering off by 2007. Yes, I am noticing this pattern as well. These waves of children in each group seem to be shorter and shorter as each group comes in. Perhaps an indication that we are getting closer and closer to the shifting of humanity.

The second wave of Rainbow children began to arrive in 2005, but really began to take off in 2007. with the last of them still trickling in at the time of this writing. These children are so similar to the Crystal children that I feel I would only be repeating myself in a greater explanation of them. However, the third group of Rainbow children who began to arrive in late 2013 and are still arriving are a bit different. While they have the same attributes as the other children, this group seems wise beyond their years. I can attest through raising my grandson that I need to treat this three-year-old almost like an adult on many occasions. He needs everything explained to him as if you are speaking to a very wise person. It's not okay to just say you are too young or get out of that. He needs it to be explained to him exactly why, and he needs things shown to him. He wants to know exactly how, and why everything works, yet he watches and listens with intent understanding. And that was at age two. He's never okay with me cooking on my own. He wants to learn how to do It and be shown. He wants to do everything for himself, and often uses large words in proper sentences. He also is very psychic in his own right and can tell me where his dad is when I have no idea where his dad is. Yet, if his dad stops at Walmart during the day, he knows his dad went to Walmart. Nobody needs to tell him because he already knows. Yes, raising a Rainbow child is quite different from other children. In place of tearing the cabinets apart at age two, he's mixing waffles and telling me how to cook them. At age three, he is thirsty and tells me he needs water in order to hydrate his body because he doesn't want to become dehydrated. This child is also a healer and before he was even able to speak, he would communicate with the plants, touching each tree or leaf for long periods of time just looking intently at it. Even now at age three, he often will stop and hold his hands over a flower and tell me he's doing energy on it. By taking a humble stance with these children, and realizing they are the teachers, we may just truly understand that we are in for a future of much spiritual advancement through these amazing souls.

My guides have mentioned that this third wave of Rainbow children are preparing us for a group that has not yet arrived, and they are called the Dragonfly kids. The third group of Rainbows, like the first group of Crystals, will often carry traits of both groups. These children are called transitional children. The children will be so much more advanced than even the Crystal and Rainbow kids are. These children will be born awake, meaning that they will remember exactly who they are, where they come from, and why they are here. They will be able to clearly teach us of the infinite creator, the different dimensions, and very advanced levels of math, science, and astronomy. I personally am finding it very interesting and exciting to think of such children arriving here in the near future.

Now about the same time as the Indigo children began to arrive in the Western hemisphere a group of children began to arrive in the east known as the super psychic children. The Chinese government had been performing their own testing on them and attempted to keep them a secret from the world, including their own country. That is until 1995 when *Paul Dong* and *Thomas Raffill* published a book titled,*"China's Super Psychics,"* bringing this to the attention of the world. Since then, there have been many documentaries and journalists who have brought more light to the subject. Currently, these children are incarnating at such a high rate they are unable to even build schools fast enough to accommodate them. And it is no longer possible to keep them a secret.

These are children who can speak over 100 languages fluently by age four, born to parents who cannot speak more than one, or teach math to a college professor by age five. There is a little boy who can see perfect in pitch black darkness, even better than in any type of light, including sunlight. In another instance they filled a ball stadium with spectators. Each one of them holding a rose bud while a small girl stood in the center of the field. She bloomed each rose bud simultaneously with a wave of her hand. Sounds like superhero stuff movies are made out of, right? These children are not incarnating in a certain location by accident, so of course I had to ask my guides as to why they were all over there. I was told they had to balance out the Indigo and Crystal children being born on the other side of the planet. Not only that, but they have an important job to do, and yes, I asked what that job was. I was informed that we do not need to know what that job is for the time being, because we will all know without a doubt when the time comes.

What does it mean to be a Star child or a Star Seed and what is the difference? This is quite simple. These advanced children are often called Star children or Star Seeds meaning that the Star children simply advanced themselves in another location meaning on another planet and agreed to come here during this great time of change as an advanced soul. This simply means they didn't originate here for their advancement. They are known by many names. Psychic and author *Sylvia Brown* referred to them as Mystic travelers and in the, *"Law of One Series," by Carla Rueckert, Don Elkins and James McCarty*, the RA is a group of advanced consciousness who channeled through *Carla Rueckert*. And in this book the RA refers to them as the wanderers while here we have been calling them Indigo, Crystal and Rainbows.

The difference between a Star child and a Star seed means that a Star seed is a child who has extra-terrestrial DNA. And, yes, I am aware that we all do, each, and every human on the planet has extra-terrestrial DNA. However, the Star Seeds had their DNA changed while still in utero and their star family is not quite so distant as the rest of us. They truly do have more than the traditional two human parents that the rest of us have. Also, I have been told through the guides that many of these DNA upgrades that happen during pregnancy often take place while the mother is sleeping, and she may never see, or feel, it happening, they do it on another plane meaning in the spirit form. No, they do not kidnap the mother, take her on a spaceship and entice horrible fear in her while she is pregnant. When you hear stories such as this, they are of a negative origin and not of these loving spiritual beings just making adjustments to the fetus in order for their contracted wanderer to be able to live and survive in the new third dimensional body they are trying to inhabit. Some of these negative experiences may also be connected to government secret programs. This is not a conspiracy book, so I will go no further on this other than to say that just because a child is created in this manner doesn't mean there is anything wrong with them. And it doesn't mean they are a negative soul either.

These kids often have extra-terrestrial encounters starting at a young age that might include dreams, visions, memories or, literally, a craft often arriving at their home for frequent visits. These experiences often occur throughout their lifetime, and generally it's not limited to childhood only. These children often have extra-terrestrials as guides, and in many cases the mother will have an unusual pregnancy to include many bazaar lucid dreams. Keep in mind this is not limited to my brief descriptions here.

These children are often psychic and have many traits of the Indigo, Crystal and Rainbow kids. In many cases, at least one parent had some sort of government or military connection. These children are not to be feared. They are not here to breed us out and take us over. They have been doing this for thousands of years. They are here to help us upgrade, so to speak, both our DNA, and our spiritual connection with source, and will prepare us for the coming changes to humanity and the world. These children are here to bring their love and light to brighten our way into ascension. I am in no way an expert on the Star children but what I do know is that they, be it the soul or the soul plus genetic manipulation, often feel like they don't belong here, like they just have this knowing that this is not their home; the planet, lifetime, location, time or whatever nothing ever seems to fit. They commonly feel a need to leave this lifetime and go "home" wherever that may be. The negative energy of this planet is very difficult for them to live in, and they often struggle with living in such a low vibratory place. They often have allergies because they are attempting to adapt to a foreign environment. I recommend the book, *"Journal of a Star Seed," by Charis Brown Malloy*, if you are interested in understanding more about the star kids.

I also would like to mention that my guide Emily has made it quite clear that as we make such a fuss over these advanced wandering souls who are shaking up the world, we are missing out on one great piece of information and that is the human souls who have been here from the beginning. They are the ones who have done all the footwork to prepare their planet for this shift, and it's their ancestors to include themselves in past lives that got us this far. These souls are so advanced that they have similar, if not the same attributes, as the Indigo children and most of the ones being born today often are thought to be Indigo children. However, they are not wanderers. This is their planet and they are here to shift it!

Regardless of what group a child or adult is categorized in, we know one thing is for certain, we are doing them all a great disservice by categorizing them. This does nothing but feed the ego and gives a false sense of self-worth that puts one above the other and the need for superficial attention seeking. This is spiritually crippling for all of us. Leave the drama and Hollywood sensationalism out of the stories of what they are experiencing. Drama is nothing short of destruction to everyone involved. It creates closed ears and over-reactive emotions. By giving our children a balanced, grounded and healthy sense of self, we can give our children the tools they need to be the change in the world they came here to be.

Imagine what these children will accomplish as well-developed adults? Honestly, their capabilities far exceed our ability to imagine such greatness. And true greatness is shared, it cannot be accomplished with a select few being led to believe they are more special than the others, or if a large group is neglected to the point that depression and darkness is at the forefront.

Remember, these advanced kids and psychic kids are all still kids and they need to still be treated as such. They need to be loved, encouraged, and supported. Support their hobbies and interests, as well as their dreams and desires. Above all, our children need to be acknowledged and listened to. I mean, truly and deeply listen to them and what they have to say. Take it in with true intent, and without fear, doubt or discord. The dysfunctional ideas of our parents and grandparents have no room in the way we raise the children of our future. Clearly, it didn't work too well for the last 100 generations and it certainly has no chance of working in a positive manner for the new group of humans who have come here to improve the planet and all who reside here. But one thing is for certain, we are all here for something big that is happening right now before our very eyes, and it is a very exciting time to be here right now.

CHAPTER THREE

EXTRA TERRESTRIALS

I debated on adding this into my book but since I explained the difference between Star kids and the Star Seeds, I decided I had to add this chapter. At first being quite challenged to simplify, and minimize into only one chapter, but thanks to my niece Taylor, I think I got it. My entire goal here is to bring some level of understanding, while minimizing the fear factor.

One of the most important things I want you to know, without a doubt, is that they are not here to steal all our natural resources and leave the planet a dead empty waste. We are doing a good enough job of that on our own. And besides, do you really think they are still using natural resources with all the technology they possess? I mean it is crazy that we are even still using them ourselves. And, no, they are not here to take over the planet in the way that some people might perceive with them openly running everything while we would become their minuscule slaves. The truth is we are all slaves, but mostly to our own mind. And, they are absolutely not here to "breed" us out, while replacing us with their own species. On that subject, the reality is that they have been manipulating our DNA for thousands of years and we already are the alien species they have created. Think that's a crazy far-fetched idea? At one, point humans and Neanderthals lived side-by-side. We did not evolve from them yet we all, yes, that means all, of us, have somewhere between 1 and 3% Neanderthal DNA. Yet, nobody really knows what happen to them. And, at one point all humans had brown hair, brown eyes, and brown skin. Then, randomly there was a male born with blue eyes about ten thousand years ago and every blue-eyed person on the planet can trace their history to that person. At this point they call it a random mutated gene. If you still believe things happen randomly, then it's a good thing you are reading this book. Because nothing in creation is random. Then we have green eyes, the, most rare eye color in the world, and if you do an Internet search you will find conflicting information regarding where it originated, however every ethnicity on the planet has green-eyed people. While if you look around the world you will find that someone from the African Congo looks quite different than someone from Japan, Ireland, or South America. Do you really mean to tell me that everyone came from Africa and just mutated into looking quite different from each other purely at random? Or their skin turned so white from migrating into a cloudy and snowy climate requiring more clothing and less sun? If that was so true, then why are there such white people in Russia at the same time there are tan skinned nomads? What about the people living in the Arctic Circle and are always covered in thick layers of animal skins, yet they have tan skin? And how come the people of Africa have darker skin than the people of South America when the climate is very similar? That story just doesn't jive, and I don't care who you are trying to sell it to, I'm not buying it. The Dogon tribe from Africa has had an oral history that tells their story of being descendants from ancestors who hail from the Dog Star long before Western astrologers had any idea there was a Dog Star. Everywhere you look China, Japan, South America, Norway, Ireland, even Native American tribes have stories of either their Gods who came down from the sky and made Demi-God children or they came to create a Star child who was born only to be taken away by age six in a flying craft back to the stars, or sometimes left here to be raised by human parents.

Now the most basic question given would be, are they good or bad? They are both just like you and me. There are basically two groups out there (actually; more but that's too much for this chapter) and both groups are made up of a large variety of beings that may look similar to us, or quite different from us, due to the fact that they come from so many different planets and origins. The Orion group is basically all negative, and yes, they do have some pretty, dastardly plans for not only us, but for people like us on many other planets as well. They are the bullies of the galaxy and tend to push their weight around. Just think galactic Nazis with advanced technology, and you will get a pretty good idea of what they are all about. However, they are not to be feared for we humans have just as much power and abilities as they do. In fact, we have more, and this frightens them. If we are not using our psychic abilities, and we believe they are bigger, badder and better than we are, they do have an upper hand. But once we, as a society, rise above the fear they attempt to create in us, they cannot do anything to us. Yes, there are cosmic laws of the universe put in play that even the negative groups must follow, although they are always looking for loopholes. However, once some of this becomes more understood by us humans, the more worried they get. It's like keeping someone uneducated for the purpose of exerting power and control over them, but once that person realizes they don't have to listen to the bully, and realize they can do whatever they want, the power of the bully seems to dissipate astronomically. Please note that not everyone who lives in the Orion Constellation have dark plans, the group calling themselves the Orion group are the ones with dark plans. Remember there are many humans on this planet who also can be seen as being dark and scary as well as light and loving.

The other group is called the Federation and they are all about peace, love, harmony, and spirituality. They are against war and fighting and only serve the positive progress of others. Think Star Trek with a love - one - another hippie twist to their agenda. It's easy to see why the negative group is here and what their agenda is but what are these guys doing here? Well, it's easy. In their past, all their different planets that they hail from have a similar past as we have with dark times, war, prejudices, and endless arguing over politics and religions. They too went through tumultuous times, like what we are going through now in order to rise above it and advance themselves into the loving spiritually advanced beings they are today. Now that they have advanced to that point, they are working towards a service to others' path, however, they have gotten to a point where their entire planet is serving each, other, and they are in need of branching out into the universe to continue finding others to serve. This is a long story, short version. But they continue to become more advanced light beings only by serving others, and this brings them great joy in doing so.

Members of the Orion group are what we call polarizing service to self and they are the true sociopaths of the galaxy, having no concerns for others, nor do they have a conscious to speak of in most cases. Only wishing to benefit themselves and, yes, even willing to sacrifice each other in the process of whatever they may gain in the process, or, in order to escape being held accountable for their actions. The more service to self-actions they perform, the more advanced they become as a dark being instead of a white being.

This is a universal process and we are every bit part of it as they are. Every entity on every planet is equally a part of this process. It's the whole good versus evil and polarizing more towards the positive or negative. With each lifetime experience being an opportunity to work more towards one or the other. If you are now asking yourself which one you happen to be, then I will tell you that you are a light being because dark beings will not ask themselves that question. If you have love and compassion in you for yourself and others to include animals, plants, and people, then you are absolutely a bright light.

Both sides of these groups have bases here on our planet and in the surrounding areas. These bases are in the ocean, deep in the earth, and inside mountains. They have a certain level of conflict going on between them, and while I am not an expert on their conflicts or their weapons, I do know that the positive side has some sort of shield that whatever you send to them in order to attack will come right back at you. In other words, they won't send you a bomb, but if you send them one it will come directly back and hit you, not them. To my understanding this is okay. For we are not allowed to do harm, or to will harm upon others, but we can reflect back to them what they send out in order to create an opportunity for them to learn from this experience.

Another question often asked is, "When will we get to meet them and see their ships?" That seems to be the big question. So many of us, including myself, keep wondering when will we get full disclosure on this subject? I think we are currently in the middle of disclosure, yet we are not seeing the forest for the trees. The television shows *"Ancient Aliens"* and *"Hanger one"* on the History Channel are full of disclosure. And let's not leave out *Dr. Steven Greer*, who not only has several books written on this subject, but two movies out right now as well. He is definitely front and center on this disclosure project. And what about more modern information? There are many authors such as *Christopher O'Brian* who wrote *"The Mysterious Valley"* and *Richard Dolan's "UFO's for the 21ˢᵗ Century."* They have definitely put their life's work into writing on a more modern-day level. As well as reporters such as *Linda Moulton Howe* and radio shows such as Coast to Coast a.m. out of California with a nationwide broadcast. Then there is Gaia T.V., which offers many shows in-regards to modern day information with expert interviewers like *George Noorey* and *David Wilcock*. Now we have insiders coming forward with much information to share like *Corey Goode,* and *Emery Smith*. One Internet search on any of these resources, and a host of information will be available to you.

Why don't these positive groups just show themselves and say, "Hey, here we are?" There are certain cosmic laws that must be followed and the law of free will is one of them. We have-to want them to show themselves. And, it can't be just a few of us. There has-to be a certain number of us on the planet who are ready and willing for it to happen, and my understanding is that we are getting close to that now. They cannot interfere with our free will, and at the same time they don't want to shock us. I mean what would happen if all of their cloaked ships just uncloaked themselves at one time in the sky? People watching Hollywood's version of space aliens would instantly think we are being attacked or want to go out and worship them like gods, which is what our ancestors did. People, steeped in religion are not ready to believe our wonderful creator created anything more than this reality, and would definitely be in for a level of shock that would require serious counseling. Some people might even become suicidal.

To know our history as we have been taught, might this knowledge be full of more inaccuracies than accurate facts and, also would create a level of confusion difficult to adjust to right away. The inaccuracies of our history are only beginning to come to light and are not in our mainstream school systems yet. One must do their own research in order to find what scholars, scientists, archeologists and researchers of ancient texts are finding, yet it's all being withheld to some extent for various reasons.

Then there's the fact that we have had the knowledge of, and regular contact with these beings, for a very long time and it has been kept from us. I mean the economy would fall, people would panic, and the stores would be wiped out in an hour. People might stop going to work and while this might not seem so disastrous in the immediate future, look at what we rely upon in our daily lives by all of us doing our part at our jobs, whether we enjoy that job or not. We are a vital part of each other's survival here. Especially anyone in the food, medical, and emergency fields.

They would like the transition to go smoothly, and I'm sure we all want the same thing whether we know it or not. It is coming, and in our near future, where we will look up and it might remind us of a scene from Star Wars where the people walking down the street will not all look like us. However, if we all knew how many extra-terrestrials are already in our daily lives, we would be shocked. Some look like us and we never think twice, while others are using a disguise in order to fit in. And, yes, you can find most of this on the Internet these days. But, please be warned, that about 90% of the Internet videos, pictures, and stories are all fake. But that should not discredit the fact that there is some authentic stuff out there and they are here. There are some unusual things people see in the sky, and it's not others just making things up. Where I live, we see UFO's on a regular basis, and my son has been getting regular contact with them in his dreams for many months now. And I have channeled several groups if them as well. More and more people will be getting dream contact the closer we get to full disclosure as a way of preparing us for this event.

What about abductions? There are two facets to these and, like everything else, we have positive and negative. One side is that some people agree to come here and be abducted, and I know this sounds crazy, right? I mean who in the world is agreeing to be abducted? If you and your people are needing some genetic material for your genetic experiments and you decide to volunteer in order to allow your group to collect what they need without breaking the laws of free will, then you might volunteer to do such a thing. Perhaps you say, "I will go and incarnate there as a human, so you can abduct me and take my DNA," and or, "I will give you a child," and so on. If you agree to something in your soul contract before you are born, you are obligated to it, and using free will as an excuse because you change your mind after the fact doesn't fly.

Then there are some people who get abducted by the negative groups this is not prearranged to my understanding, and the whole fear factor negative experiences that people come back with after they remember it, or parts of it, is simply because they want to exert power over you. Yes, they can get your DNA and blood, and whatever they want from you in a calm, painless and less intrusive manner, however, this would not suit their purpose for creating fear and the feeling of helplessness they want to entice within you.

When you hear stories of people saying that they were shown their children years later, on board a ship, or that they didn't hurt them yet took them anyway and did some testing, then returned them unharmed these are not only positive groups, they are your positive group. Therefore, they wish to do you no harm and they do things in a much kinder way than the negative groups do.

Now please don't be frightened by the fact that these beings are here. They are very much like you and me. They have families and lives and dreams and goals and feel love and joy and happiness. They are not gods like our ancestors believed them to be, and they are not better or greater than we are. We are all the same. They are of the same infinite creator as we are, and they are part of us as we are part of them, as well as each other. We are all one and they understand that better than we do. Imagine us with greater advancement in technology and spirituality. So please don't fear thousands of ships being uncloaked in our skies and, for goodness sake do not drop down on your knees and worship them as gods but welcome them, and the advancements that they bring with them like better medical care, greater spiritual understanding the elimination of poverty, and a more balanced and loving lifestyle between all of us. Think of the wondrous things they have to teach us and help us to accomplish in our future; things like eliminating cancer, depression, abuse and mental illness, not to mention bringing teleportation and space travel. Just as you would welcome a new friend from another country so should you, and all of us, welcome new friends from another planet. This chapter, by no means even begins to cover what I know in regards to this subject let alone what can easily be found by the experts so please look at this as a basic understanding in order to peak your interest enough to research more on this by the people who have dedicated decades to it.

CHAPTER FOUR

UNDERSTANDING SOUL INCARNATIONS

Have I actually lived a past life? Has everyone lived a past life? What is a new soul or an old soul? How do I know if I am an old soul? Could I have shared a past life with any of the people in this life? These are some of the most common questions I hear from people. Yes, you have lived many past lifetimes, as well as everyone you know. And yes, everyone you know, has definitely shared lifetimes with you before. Yes, you are what people consider an old soul, if there is such a thing; that would be an entity that has experienced many lifetimes as many things for many millions of years, if you wish to view time as linear which is what we are programed to do. A new soul would be an entity that has lived fewer lifetimes as fewer things, and possibly never has been human, or perhaps human for only a few lifetimes. Currently, all humans on the planet are what people often call old souls. The reason for this is because we are now at the end of the current Earth cycle, and she is shifting along with all who inhabit her into another cycle of life which is beautiful and wonderful. Therefore, only advanced souls are incarnating on the Earth right now. That means every one of you have experienced pretty much everything; like being male and female, and you have been both rich and poor, happy and tragic, killed and been killed, lived on all parts of the planet to include a variety of ethnic backgrounds as well.

We all incarnate here in what is called soul groups, therefore the people in your life are all people you have shared other lifetimes with, for sure. In all the years that I have been doing past life regressions on people, I have only come across one that I can recall who claims to have a first life experience with someone who was close to them in this lifetime. Not impossible as nothing is, however, it is very highly unusual.

How do I know all of this? I have been doing past life regressions for going on 20 years at the time of this writing, and I have yet to come across someone who has never lived a lifetime before this. We have all lived an unfathomable amount of time in the way we understand time to be. The truth is time is not linear, therefore, to measure in time is an inaccurate way of understanding the amount of time each one of us have existed, but for the sake of the human understanding I will go with it in that terminology. Time was only created to feel linear for our benefit of experience. On the Other Side we do not experience time. Everything is in the now. We come here in order to experience this dimension and reality which is to include everything it has to offer, such as time, food, relationships, difficulties, happy, sad, glad, mad, frustration, you name it, we are here to experience it. If all we experienced was an awesome, wonderful perfect life on every incarnation what would we truly experience then? While we all have had at least one lifetime full of love, happiness, and little hardship, it is rarely the case due to the fact, that the soul will not advance without a variety of obstacles to overcome. Advancement will happen but extremely slow.

As the guides have explained it to me, we all emerge out of source as a tiny, bright light and there are Angels whose sole job it is to retrieve as the baby souls emerge. They are brought from source in a gentle, pure, loving and, caring way of handling. Each soul is then watched and cared for by these Angels as they are in charge of assisting them going into and out of many lifetimes. Such as single cell organisms, fish, plants, birds, reptiles, and so on, until each soul begins to have self-acknowledgement. Once they understand the self and have matured enough, they may incarnate as a third density being Human. During the first few lifetimes they may still carry some animal characteristics from their most recent incarnation with them. And I don't mean wild, or they will attack you without a conscious type of behavior. Even animals don't behave this way.

Let's say they were a wolf last time. They may have more dedication and connection to family, aka; their pack in a way that seems more loyal than most people, even to a point where others might not understand it. This is just an example, while there are not any souls currently on the planet right now living in a human body who are not advanced enough to handle the end of the Earth age. Yes, we are all here for this big finale! This is a beautiful and remarkable thing to experience. Many people from all over the universe consider us privileged to be a part of it. Even souls on the other side who have a different role than to be here are in awe of the possibility to experience this. Yes, yes, I know, I said the same thing. ARE YOU CRAZY? This place sucks, and I do not feel privileged by being here it's more like a punishment, and what did I do wrong to be so hated by creation that I have to be here? It's much different on the other side where they view only experience as the most important thing, not the fact that the experience is so difficult. In fact, if a person chooses to stay in a difficult situation such as, depression, anxiety or self-hatred, just to give examples, they still look at it as experience, and to them a bad experience is better than no experience. And, yes, things like depression and anxiety are self-induced. Before everyone gets themselves into an uproar about this, let me just say I have had extreme anxiety to the point my legs gave out and my body stopped functioning. I have experienced extreme depression as well as PTSD, therefore, I do have a place to talk about something that I do know about first-hand.

Once a soul is ready and capable of planning and deciding their own lifetime, the Angels who cared for them through so many lifetimes as a baby soul will then turn them over to a group of very advanced loving beings to include a group called the council. At this time you also will meet Angels, as well as animal totems and guides who are all there to assist you in creating and preparing your lifetimes. Imagine parents letting their kids go off to college. That would be a similar scenario except magnify the love by thousands of times. And that is a small glimpse of what the Angels do, letting go of their charges in order for the soul to advance, while accepting more beautiful and bright baby souls to assist. At this point the soul will begin to work with their council which is a group of very advanced entities who have been around for an extremely long time in the capacity that we understand time anyway. They will assist in the planning of your next lifetime, as well as offer guidance and suggestions to help you along the way with achieving your goals of each incarnation. They work with you, your Angels and Guides (experienced human souls who have decided to expand their experiences by helping others to incarnate), and totems (our animal guides who choose to assist and help guide us in our lifetimes as well). The council is not only available for you to request knowledge and assistance from, but your guides and totems go to them for advice and direction. What did you think our guides do when they get stuck on what to do with our stubbornness after we get here and don't want to follow the plan? Yes, people do often come here and get stuck caught up in this reality then decide to change the plan once they are down here. Some people go way off course, while others do just slightly and are easily pushed back on track. How does this happen? Example: three or four times over a matter of a few years you thought about doing something big like leave your husband, or job, but decided against it. In some cases, this may be a branch and either way is fine just a different experience, however, if the life path requires you to take the plunge and make the life altering changes required in order to stay on your life path, they may take matters into their own hands and have you get fired or your spouse decided to cheat on you creating the catalyst that caused the change to happen. They don't do these devastating things as a punishment but as a way to keep you on the path you were meant to be on. At first this may very well seem like a devastating time in your life, but then in a few years you look back and say, "Hey, if that didn't happen, I never would have done this and that and look where I am today?" Also, people may often use the idea of free will to not do what is presented to them. I will tell you that you do have free will and you did exercise that free will when you wrote this life with the assistance and guidance of your guides and Angels. You did give them permission to assist in keeping you on that path therefore they are not taking away, or interfering with, your free will by creating a situation to push you into the situation that will get you back on your life path. They do this out of love and not out of getting you back for not listening.

I have come across people who have advanced past the animal incarnation stage, lived many, human lives, only to request other lifetimes as an animal for various reasons. My current dog, Keeva, is one such soul. My Guide Emily asked her to, or I should say the way Emily stated it, "I contracted Keeva for you." Keeva is a very advanced soul who agreed to come share some of this lifetime with me as my dog friend and healer. Yes, she is a healing soul and whenever I am working in my healing room, she insists on being in there with me when I am working.

We continue to reincarnate as a third density being i.e.; human or the like either on this planet or another third density planet until which time we are ready to advance into a fourth density being and so on and so on. If you are wondering what the densities are just think of it like school. You must go through each grade in order to graduate into the next grade and so goes it for soul experience but think of each life as only part of that grade until you have experienced it enough to be prepared to move on. And, you literally may have lived thousands of lifetimes in each density before advancing into the next density. As you move on you become more loving and spiritual with a greater understanding of the spiritual self, as well as your spiritual connection with your soul group, with each level of advancement and a greater understanding of our infinite creator and your spiritual place among the entire universal experience. This is a very simplistic explanation of a very complex subject. If you are more interested in how this works, I recommend reading, *"The Law of One,"* series already mentioned in this book. As well as *"The Source Field Investigations," by David Wilcock.*

We all experience an enormous number of lifetimes in each density, and become ready to graduate into another density. Then we can become what the universe refers to as a wanderer, and we humans refer to them as Star children. These wanderers can travel lateral, or below them, but not to an advanced location. For example, you become a fourth-density human and after a few lifetimes you start to think that you might want to visit other planets and locations around the universe. At that point you may wander, or incarnate, on any fourth density or third density planet you wish to visit in order to expand your experience. And yes, a fourth density entity can decide to incarnate on a third density planet and that planet would look at them as an advanced child. A fifth or sixth density entity arrives, and he is known as a master teacher, or a miracle worker or prodigy child and so forth. To be a wanderer is nothing more than expanding your experience further through traveling to other locations for experience. Think university studies in other countries after taking a few courses closer to home.

What about in-between? Yes, there is a very important part in between lives. We go to the other side where we originated from after each incarnation. In short, it goes something like this… exit your body, return home to an amazing homecoming party. I have heard so many times, "I don't want to die alone," or, "I'm afraid to die alone." I assure you that nobody dies alone, ever. For at that moment the soul leaves the body, it's a very peaceful and loving moment. As that soul continues forth to the Other Side, they become more and more aware of their surroundings, where they are and why they left to incarnate as a human. They begin to remember things forgotten, like who they are and where they came from and why they are here. There are always Angels to assist, as well as your spirit guides, totems, pets and loved ones from this lifetime and from other lives. All are ready and waiting to greet you in an abundance of love, joy and gratitude for the reunion. Then we go through what is called orientation, which is a process in reacquainting you into your surroundings. You and your guides discuss the lifetime you just experienced, as well as healing. The healing is done by both Angels and humans who are very experienced in helping damaged souls who arrive home with traumas and emotional pain from the current lifetime. Sometimes souls are so damaged upon arrival that they are put into healing pods. How I see them is like a butterfly cocoon and it literally folds around them when they enter it and enter a sleep-like state as the emotional damage is healed and repaired. How long someone would stay varies, depending upon the soul itself, and since time doesn't exist anyway it isn't really measured by time. How long a loved one is in the healing pod could be measured by our time, I suppose, however it is difficult to make a fair comparison. They may take weeks or months or years, all the while loved ones on this side are anxiously awaiting a sign or message from them. When this is the case, remember some may be in a healing pod while some may be preparing for another incarnation or busy back at their regular occupations. Just give it a while because a day or week or month or year is all the same to them.

Once a soul is re-oriented to their environment they may go on a vacation (yes, we can go on vacation over there) anywhere they would like to go. Perhaps somewhere here on Earth, or perhaps a location over there, or even another planet. Nothing is impossible. Then they go back to work and perhaps skip the vacation part. Yes, we do work over there but it's not like here. We are required to work in order to make money and pay bills, which creates stress, and we do a variety of things for a job even if we are unhappy with it to ensure rent is paid. This is not true over there. Over there we have no money, no bills and no going without anything you want or need. You never work a job you don't absolutely love, and you put all your love into it. Perhaps you are a healer or assist babies in the process of incarnation. I personally am a researcher on the Other Side, which makes sense because I'm an avid researcher in this life as well.

At some point each one of us will decide to go back into another lifetime. This is for more reasons than I can come up with. Think about it. We are close to reaching eight billion people on this planet, and that means each one of us has a different and unique story and reason for being here. Sure, there are some general and common reasons, but each one is a unique soul and every lifetime is unique unto itself. Perhaps we already planned many lifetimes out at once. Perhaps a friend asked us to come in and be a major part of their lifetime. Perhaps the council asked us to go in and accomplish certain things. Whatever the reason, we decide to come here and are still required to prepare, which entails writing up a script. Your script is a plan you write out for your pending lifetime to include all the people in your life experience and many branches to give you many choices to take while here. The people you choose to have in your life are also people who have chosen you. They are people that you have shared many lifetimes and many different situations. You know them, they are your soul group, and yes, we incarnate in soul groups. I'm told that we first find our group by matched frequencies. Imagine you are a being made up of pure energy and you travel at a frequency that makes beautiful music unique only to you. Yes, for every soul out there we each have our own frequency. Isn't that beautiful and amazing? We attract to others who travel at a certain frequency band that matches ours. This is where we establish our soul group or soul family. We may incarnate together as family members, friends, coworkers, mentors, you name it. Even a brief run in for only a few minutes, or a day, is a wonderful spiritual encounter with a good friend from the Other Side. Just because our encounter was brief doesn't mean it was not a plan written into your life chart for varied reasons.

Just because you shared a past life doesn't mean this person is meant to be your spouse for the entirety of this lifetime. Your soul mate is your soul group. They are all your soul mates and you have been friends, siblings, lovers and enemies in many lifetimes. It doesn't mean you wrote it in this time. There are many soul mates out there and you will find them wherever you look once you take the romantic connotation out of it.

Do we all have what is called a twin flame? And if so, what is a twin flame? The answer to that is yes, as far as my understanding goes. As we emerge from source, we are divided into two. Like when identical twins develop, they begin as a single egg but quickly split into two halves of the same soul. On very rare occasions I have come across a set of three, so you could be part of a triplet flame. While there is not really such a thing as a gender on that side, there is such a thing as energy. And these two halves will always be one male energy and one female energy. They do not always incarnate together at the same time! You will either meet your twin flame, or you will not in this lifetime, so to go looking for your other half is absolutely a waste of your time. Also, while I know some people are insistent that twin flames are always romantic partners, I must tell you that I have two friends who met their twin flames much later in life and they were not romantic partners. I myself have met mine and trust me, it is not all that it's cracked up to be. In both occasions for my friends the energies were so strong and bazaar there was absolutely no doubt this was a twin flame situation. Both had been in long-term relationships with their spouses with grown children and grandchildren. Romance was not an option and not even scheduled to be so. However, there was much spiritual growth on both sides through the connection of these souls here on this plane.

Before you come back into another lifetime here you will agree to what is called a soul contract. Each person who will be guiding you from the other side or is to share any part of your life with you on this side, will be written into this contract. Your soul contract is binding and while you must experience the people in your life that you agreed to share it with, you do have some options. Example: If someone is toxic be it a family member, spouse, friend or coworker, then you do have the right and ability to cut all ties to them if it is service to your higher good and advancement. However, you must release them with love and not negativity or resentment. Some people may need to take time away from that person in order to heal before they find the love in their heart to project love towards them and let it go. That doesn't mean let them back in your life. That means come to terms with the situation and send love energy through your thoughts and emotions towards them and say, "I release you of your soul contract with me to include all karmic ties or debt between us," then, with pure love in your heart and good intensions for that person release them from your life and your thoughts. Regardless of how terrible they have been to you it is never okay to wish them ill will. It is not necessary to tell them in person, nor do they even need to know you have done this in order to separate with pure love intentions. Go to an alone and quiet place to do this. It must come from love though, or it will not work. It doesn't matter what they did to you, or if they got theirs in the end. It only matters that you have grown spiritually past it. This is for your soul advancement not theirs.

After you plan your life and sign all your soul contracts, you will go visit your council and they will review your script while offering their expert advice and suggestions of any changes they believe should be done. Ultimately, you do have the final say on whether you wish to adhere to their advice. At some point, you will see a counselor type person who is to oversee the finalization of your life script. I personally remember being in a huge Romanesque-type building with monolithic pillars made of white marble and it was absolutely beautiful. As we walked down the center isle which was huge, I noticed that on either side between the pillars was a desk with a person sitting on the opposite side of it, while a guide with soon to be new incarnates was on the near side facing this person and talking. While we have many guides, we usually have one or two who are the closest, or main guides, and in this building only the contracted soul with one guide seem to be present. I went with my guide, Emily, and we walked all the way to the end and at the last desk on the right we spoke with a woman. While I do not remember the entire conversation in detail, I do recall this lady attempting to convince me that this lifetime would be too difficult, and I would be at high risk of not finishing. Particularly the part where I had to do everything alone. Literally surrounded by friends and a huge family, yet no help to be had from the smallest of needs to the largest. I had no one ever to help me. By the time I was a toddler I knew I was on my own, and don't bother asking or expecting someone to help. I insisted, with all my divine feminine power that makes up my essence, that I can handle it with the attitude that I can take on the world by myself. Believe me, I remember saying this with a lot of confidence and attitude. Once this memory showed up, I was like, "wow," I do have that attitude in me that has showed up on rare occasions, and I have had to admit that I wrote this mess myself. Then I got here and said screw this, I want out. In fact, I have spent most of my life wanting out and I did have to admit to my guides that they were right, and I was wrong, and this is much more difficult than I predicted. Talk about having to humble myself and admit that everyone else was correct. I was thinking I could handle such a big load that I was not prepared to handle. But here I am, for now, anyway.

Once your decisions have all been made, then it is time to incarnate here. There are Angels and humans who assist in helping the souls incarnate into the next lifetime. My nephew, Kyle, once told his Mom, my sister, that he distinctly remembers waiting to be born and feeling very excited and anxious awaiting his turn to go. He said he was a grown man and then he was told it was his turn to come here. His next memory was being an infant. Then, once we are here, we are to live out our life contracts with all our soul family who has agreed to be here with us, as well as our pets. Once we arrive here, we have forgotten who we are during the birthing process. While some of our memories from the other side are retained, most of our memories are forgotten at this time. Yes, the connection to the other side is still strong but, it continues to fade as our time here grows. Generally, between the ages of five and seven is about the time the complete forgetting happens. We have an army of helpers on the Other Side helping us with this new adventure, yet, we have totally forgotten who they are, how we know them as well as why we have chosen them, or they have chosen us, and we agreed. We are subjected to a wide variety of beliefs, schools, religions, culture, as well as judgments and social structures that don't really exist on the Other Side. It is completely foreign to us and we learn from our environment to develop our own constructs based on such things since our memories of the other side are so blocked. It is our job to remember who we are, where we came from and why we are here. Wow, what a job to do! I assure you that you are on your path of remembering because otherwise you would not be reading this. Just think of your memories as a jigsaw puzzle with a piece showing up here or there for you to put the puzzle together again. And, what does the puzzle look like when putting it together? There may be a corner done, an edge or part of an edge, random pieces in the center and so on. This is how your puzzle will get built and your remembering will show up more and more until you have the complete picture and understanding of who you are and why you are here. Yes, you do have an important role to play in the entire grand scheme of it all.

CHAPTER FIVE

UNDERSTANDING GHOSTS, SPIRITS AND DARK ENTITIES

Ghosts, spirits and soul self; now here is a subject that always seems to be taboo and not to be discussed on a serious basis outside of a few scary stories designed only to frighten people (which we should never do by the way, even for entertainment or joking) and pass the time as mere entertainment or old wife's tales. Many think the subject is not to be taken on any level of seriousness for fear of mocking and rejection. Or, we have the entire opposite direction to go where people find it a novelty and fun to either attend haunted locations or watch it on television (which is usually fake by the way) and find some level of entertainment.

I am not here to simply offer ghost stories or promote fear of the subject to anyone. My agenda is simply to help create a level of understanding in order to eliminate the fear and negative connotation that goes along with this subject matter.

First off, ghosts or paranormal experiences fall into many categories and figuring out who you are dealing with will eliminate half of the confusion and misunderstanding on the matter. Society-through books, movies, religion, stories and cultural-ideas has created fear and a completely unrealistic idea about who and what ghosts and spirits are. I strongly discourage anything that promotes fear on this subject, regardless of where the source comes from. That means leave Hollywood behind indefinitely on this matter, as well as any dogmatic religious ideas of such things that will cause any level of fear whatsoever.

I think I will start by saying that ghosts are people too, and there really is no need to fear them. In many cases you may not even be dealing with a ghost at all so, let's start with the non-ghost paranormal. So, who are the ghosts that are not ghosts? Perhaps you have a loved one who has crossed over and that person likes to visit regularly. Spirits are those who have crossed over and are fully aware of who they are and why they are visiting you, but once this person completely integrates into their true soul self on the Other Side they are not necessarily considered spirit but soul, however, we tend to call them spirit anyway, and to avoid more confusion, I too refer to them as spirit. Quite often you may know they are visiting. I can't tell you how many times I have seen a social media post that says, "I wish heaven had visiting hours," well it does. Loved ones come to visit regularly, and they are not earth-bound spirits also known as ghosts. Here's some wonderful news, you visit them regularly also. How? Through astral travel, of course. Yes, we all take a walk in the night while the physical body is sleeping and go to so many different places, the Other Side to visit loved ones just happens to be one of the many places we may visit.

Most often when your loved ones visit, they really wish to get your attention, not to creep you out or haunt you but to bring love, feelings of comfort or to let you know that they are alright. Mostly, they would like for you to know not to worry about them. They often leave coins in odd or bazaar places that don't make sense. My nephew said manifesting pennies to drop was easy and one of the first things he first mastered over there. So, I was all like, "Then why not manifest some dollars?" I didn't really get a reply to my sarcastic remark. Loved ones visiting may leave things out to let you know it's them, like a photo or token, that would let you know without a doubt it was them who left it right where you would find it. They may even leave doors open, or move the mirror that belonged to them, or continuously play their favorite song or band on the radio. How do you know it was them and not just the song happens to be playing on the radio? Did you immediately think of that person? Or perhaps you were thinking of them and then turned on the radio or went into a store and there was their song? My nephew played a song on the radio for my sister and she decided to test it, so she changed the station. Three stations playing the same song. Really? Perhaps you often smell their perfume or aftershave lotion or favorite flower? All these things are intended to get your attention and get you to think about them, so you know that they were visiting. This is not a haunting, but simply a visit from someone who loves you very much. See, zero creep factor involved, and these visits should not only be welcomed but cherished for the wonderful connection they really are.

Sometimes ghosts are not really ghost's but are currently inhabiting a third-dimensional body. In fact, many of them are us. That's right, you and me. You see when we astral travel during our sleep at night we don't just go to the Other Side. We also travel here on Earth. This can be our current time, or literally any time from past, present or future because time is not linear. Time was created to seem linear for our benefit of experience here in this reality. Here's just one of my own astral travel experiences where the people believed they experienced something paranormal, and I suppose they did, but, it was just me traveling in my sleep. I left my body and arrived on a street corner that was wet as if it had just rained. The buildings were that of late 1800's early 1900's and immediately upon my arrival I exclaimed to myself, "I'm in Florida!" and proceeded directly across the street to a familiar pet shop and inquired about a bird my sister and I had as a pet, but unfortunately were unable to keep, so we had taken our bird here to find him a home. We both loved this bird very much and I believe he was some type of parrot. After a detailed discussion with the store owner about who currently has my bird, I decided to go directly across the street to a very familiar building. It was the home and veterinary office of a good friend of mine, but she was not there at the time of my arrival. It was very unusual for a woman to be in her own veterinary practice in this time period, and I am uncertain of the details surrounding how her career and office/house came to be. But I do know she only cared for small animals like dogs and cats, and exotic birds. As I stated, she was not home so I decided to wait for her. At this point, I laid down on a couch and rested while I waited for her to return. During this time, I astral traveled again out of my astral form. Yes, I split into two astral forms. While my first astral form was sleeping, my second astral form shrunk down and proceeded to explore a series of doll houses she kept as a hobby. Suddenly, I was startled by hearing her screams. At this point, I was instantly pulled back into my original astral form and jolted awake as my body literally jumped from the impact of my two astral selves colliding so quickly. At this point, I heard she was screaming at a man that I was completely familiar with, and I just knew the situation from my own memory. They had been engaged, but he was a bully and verbally abusive to her, so she called off the wedding. He was trying to muscle his way into her bedroom as she was holding the door with great struggles to keep him out. She wasn't yelling for help, as nobody else was in the house to offer her any. She was yelling at him that she didn't love him anymore and to go away. I had overpowering feelings of wanting to protect her, with zero tolerance for any of his crap, as I literally merged both astral bodies and flew through her house like the ghost that I apparently was at the time. I went right through her body and the door she was struggling to close, as he was on the other side, pushing it open despite her efforts. They both immediately became aware of my presence as I came barreling through. He became instantly terrified as he ran into the room across the hall cowering and scared of me as I screamed at him. "Gilbert Greer you cannot run from me because I know who you are." He absolutely saw and heard me and became so frightened he was literally cowering in the corner as I approached. She thought I was her guardian Angel coming to protect her, while he thought I was some sort of demon after him. At this point, I instantly got pulled back into my body of this lifetime and this dimension, with full memories and understanding of what I just experienced. This was not just a past life I lived but also an alternate reality from our current one, like another dimension and time of a past life. I did have a real physical body in that lifetime, living in that reality just the same as I am here in this one right now. I visited this reality and saved my friend then came back, with full comprehension of it. I didn't even know this was possible at the time. It was this experience that taught me this is possible, and it does happen. So, for these two people they have a very intense ghost story to tell and all the while the ghost is me from another time and dimension. Most likely she even shared the story with my unknowing self of that reality.

All astral travel ghost stories are not quite so dramatic though. On another occasion I astral travelled to a small mountain town in Colorado off I-70. It was dark and snowing and I didn't know when or where I was until I saw a newspaper vending machine, I read the date on the newspaper and recognized the newspaper to be the Rocky Mountain News (which is no longer in publication). I don't remember the day, but I absolutely remember the month and year, February of 1989. I thought about where the younger version of me is, and I urgently wanted to get to myself and give instructions on certain things to do and not to do because it would create immeasurable hardships for myself in the future. My desire to bring this message was overwhelming, and I was feeling desperate to get to my apartment where I was living at the time in Aurora, Colorado, a suburb of Denver. I felt that this had to happen immediately, so I didn't think twice about hitchhiking a ride with a truck driver. As we headed down the mountain towards Denver on that snowy night, I got pulled back into my body to my own despair. I was so upset, that I was unable to take the opportunity to tell myself to fix so much of my life path, that I woke up in an emotional state that took a few days to iron out. And, I am certain the truck driver was surprised as he realized his hitchhiker disappeared right there next to him. He just looked over and I was gone. Which leads me to believe that my own ghost adventure is probably not the only disappearing hitchhiker story that's really someone astral traveling, rather than an actual ghost.

Another situation of an astral traveling ghost is my grandson. I don't even know how many times now I have heard him wake up from his nap, run around the house and even slam doors. I go to check on him only to find he's sound asleep. His astral travels only included the upstairs of the house on these particular occasions, so again, ghostly encounters, that are not really ghosts at all, may very well be an astral traveling someone from another time or reality or even a family member or someone astral traveling from our current time frame. These situations most likely won't be a repeat incident. However, that is not necessarily always the case, hence, I said most likely. There's nothing you can really do about these incidents, if this is what you have or are experiencing. It just is, and they are not out to hurt or scare you, or anyone else.

Now moving on to Earth - bound entities, or what we commonly refer to as ghosts. I want to emphasize here that while there are literally millions of confused souls that are living all over this planet, the actual amount of people who stay behind is phenomenally low. There are so many things that can cause someone to stay behind, rather than move forward and cross over. In most cases, they are simply confused as to what is going on and really have no idea, they have left their body. They no longer live in linear time as we do, so 150 years let's say is just a moment to them. So, do not keep yourself bound to the idea of, "It's been so long why haven't they figured it out yet?" Because to them it's all the same. Some of these people do stay by choice and then get confused once they decided to stay behind. It might be what people here call unfinished business, but in truth there really is not unfinished business. If a soul leaves the body all business is finished. But here is an example of what unfinished business might be. I had a friend who I was doing some bookkeeping for his business in 2008. He was building a custom home on property in Milliken, Colorado, and every day I went out behind the house and there was a man named Eric dressed in 1800's clothing who was quite confused as to what was happening on his property. Now you can't shock people by simply saying, "You're dead, cross over, go to the light, goodbye." I mean, if I told you this very thing right this minute, what would your reaction be? Say, "Okay," and run to the first light you see? I don't think so. It's no different for them. You see we don't stop being ourselves the minute we exit our bodies, and everyone deserves to be treated with love and respect. This is a delicate matter and we should all think therapy with a lot of love involved when dealing with them. So as the weeks went on, I would go talk to him daily and befriended him. Building trust is very important, especially with him, because he told me he didn't trust people since nobody would talk to him for all his efforts of communication. I learned a lot about him during our visits. He was curious as to what we were building so I told him it was a house. He thought it was the strangest house he ever saw. I invited him to go look at it, but he refused. He said it wouldn't be proper to enter a house with me, him being a man and I was a woman. I know he did eventually go inside since a guest was staying there, who was a bit rattled in the morning as he told us a story of a male ghost who opened the door and walked in the house, went past his room and down the hall. I was quite pleased Eric finally decided to come check out the house. The workmen were always complaining about their tools being moved and some materials they left in the garage overnight was in a different location the very next morning. With continued communication, I realized he stayed behind out of the love he has for his family. He was worried about taking care of them. This area was unsettled and quite dangerous, causing him to make the decision to stay with his family and farm in order to look after them. He had a daughter who I believed was about 13 at the time of his death. She was very sensitive and quite aware of her father's constant presence. He also left behind her younger brother and a wife. With different tribes of Native Americans that traveled through there, along with traders, trappers, and a variety of who knows who, he had a true and valid reason to be concerned for their safety and felt that he just had to stay in order to protect them. He was in disbelief when I told him what year it was and that his family is no longer there. How I convinced him that I was telling him the truth was by walking him around the property and showing him the tractor, truck, skid steer, and horse trailer, as I explained what they were and that these things had not been invented yet when he was living there. This did get him contemplating what I had to say, plus he was able to see my guide, Emily, who he thought was a ghost following me around. I explained to him who she was, and he finally agreed to go with her to the Other Side. I am happy to announce that he successfully crossed over.

Some people just exit their body in such a traumatic or scary way that they don't realize they left their body and are very confused. For example, I lived in a house inhabited by so many people (ghosts) I don't even know what all was going on, but there were two children there amongst them. Molly, who was very sad, and followed people around, but mostly she followed me because she was longing for a mother figure and I filled that role for her. I guessed her to be about five-or six-years-old at the time, I often babysat my friend's little girl, who was about Molly's age, and the two of them played together quite often. In fact, while I felt her, and she often followed me around, it was not me who figured out Molly's situation, it was Katie. One day they were sitting in my hallway playing together, and Katie became quite concerned for her friend Molly. She came to me right away with deep concern for Molly, saying that Molly was very frightened. When I asked why, she said Molly was surrounded by fire. A few days later an old farmer came to deliver a truckload of hay and told me a story about the original house burning down on my property, and when they rebuilt the new one burned down as well. He said the land remained empty and up for sale for many years because people believed the property to be cursed. Finally, the property sold, and my house was built there in 1954. The odd thing is I never spoke to him again, I seemed to have misplaced his phone number, and a future hay contact, which resulted in never seeing him again. Anyway, Molly was the first one I successfully crossed over and it was purely by accident. I was feeling particularly grouchy and on edge that day while she was following me as per her usual routine. However, when she did this my entire back would tingle like millions of needles poking me and it doesn't feel very comfortable. Finally, I yelled at her that I am not her Mommy and her Mommy has crossed over and she needs to go into the light in order to find her because I am not it. This hurt Molly's feelings deeply, and me being an empath and clairsentient, her emotions hit me very hard and hurt me deeply. She did cross over that very minute though, running from my meanness, I guess. I did feel sad over the situation that I hurt her so deeply, but my guide assured me that she finally was able to become healed and happy. It was not for me to feel bad about anymore because, ultimately, that was really the best thing for her and where she belongs. A few years later, I was able to help her brother Josh, who was maybe 14, cross over as well. He was shy compared to his outgoing and friendly sister, but he loved my dogs and we were able to talk and bond over the dogs. Then I was able to talk him into crossing over in a much nicer way, I'm happy to say.

Some people also might stay behind because of dogmatic belief systems put in place either by cultural or religious fears imposed upon them their entire lifetime. Perhaps you were taught that if you are a bad person you will be suffering in a place called purgatory or a fiery pit of hell for all eternity, while drilling into your mind that you are not and never will be good enough to go to a life of eternal bliss and happiness? Easy to see where people become too frightened to move forward if they have made a few mistakes and have not forgiven themselves for it. They literally become too frightened to see what awaits them on the Other Side and refuse to move forward. This happened to my father. While he was alive the fear of eternal damnation never seemed to affect him enough to not be a truly evil and self-serving abusive person, once he left his body the fear of what awaited him hit deep enough to cause him, instead, to return to his house and remain as a ghost for perhaps a year or so until the neighbor, who was also a sensitive, came over and did a clearing. He told her he was frightened to go, yet she made him leave when she did her clearing. Several years later I found out he had reincarnated to Nigeria.

There are some ghosts who stick around because they know they left their body and enjoy their life as a ghost. This is an extremely unusual situation in my experience, yet, it can happen and generally they are not nice people. Nasty in life, nasty in what we consider death (which doesn't exist by the way). You see, people don't change the minute they leave their body. If your loved one was a caring, giving and kind person in life so are they after, even if they get confused for some reason and stay behind. If they were hateful and nasty, then so too are they as a ghost. I experienced a ghost who seemed to be such a person in life. As a ghost she seemed to be not only content in her situation as a ghost, but she seemed to be elated.

A friend of mine had contacted me to come over and assist in a situation with her three-year-old son. He played regularly with an old man who he referred to as "the man," of who seemed to have taken on a loving Grandpa role towards the little boy but scared her son very deeply. One night her son was screaming in terror as he ran down her hallway and into her bedroom saying, "the man the man"! He was so traumatized by what he witnessed that he refused to sleep in his own bed for months and was unable to even relay what had happened.

My psychic daughter and I had gone over to her house the day after she called to see what answers we could get for her. As it turned, out the old man was a farmer from the area who had disappeared in 1971. His daughter who was accurately considered a suspect by the police, had murdered him in the most brutal and disgusting way. She then dismembered the body and buried him in several different farm fields in the area. My friend's property was one of where his head and torso had been buried resulting in him staying at this location. It had something to do with greed and a land inheritance.

As fate would have it, she was killed six months later when she was hit by a car. The house my friend lived in was built six years later with his remains left in her back field, not too far from the house. At this point, the daughter, who was a very dark soul, had decided that being a ghost was a good time and she often would stay in the house that had been hers in life. But she also visited his old house and several others in the area, because she believed they were now all hers and having ownership of them (in her mind anyway) was her ultimate goal from all of this. All the houses were ones she had connections to during her life, which was her reason for continuing to visit them. She only went back to the location her father was at, so she could relive the murder she committed, because she did take great pleasure in doing it. That meant this nice old man had to relive it repeatedly each time. And this is what my friends three-year-old little boy witnessed; not something a child should see. My daughter and I together managed to get rid of her, with plenty of help from our ethereal friends in the Angel realm. Now she can no longer terrorize her father, or anyone else who occupies the houses that she had laid claim to.

Unfortunately, the old man was so frightened that, for all my efforts, I was unable to get him to talk with me. He often hid in the closets and would pass through them as I had to travel around. He's deeply traumatized and had to be dealt with in a pure and loving manner. I was unable to assist in getting him to cross over due to his fear of me and constant hiding. Finally, years later I was able to learn how to cross him over without his cooperation.

This takes me to a huge peeve of mine and that would be ghost hunting groups. I know its only ignorance and curiosity that drives them, and I know I should be more understanding as to why they do it, but, admittedly, it is a challenge for me to do so. I seem to have more patience for the ghosts than the groups who are harassing them. They literally are going into locations and are abusing people in the worst way. Each, and every soul should be treated with love and compassion. What I mean is if you are not willing to go into a hospice and harass people on their death beds, as they are sick and dying, or go into a mental hospital and harass the people dealing with trauma, then why in creation is it perfectly acceptable to harass these same people after they leave their body? Do you want someone to come into your home and be all up in your grill asking ridiculous questions when you are sick, hurt or traumatized? Well, neither do they. Perhaps they don't want to talk to the people doing this because they are being loud, rude, obnoxious and annoying? If I were a ghost, I would be pretty upset by this behavior, and perhaps, I might start acting out and making the home situation worse myself, which is often what happens. Understand that these people don't experience time, so these groups going into a very active location every few weeks, or even months apart, seems to them like its constant, over, and over again, someone picking on them. They are human beings with human emotions, and they do get angry and have the right to do so, just like you or me. And, like us they may not always direct that anger in an appropriate way. Instead they might throw something or slam something. Some of these people are stuck in what's called their death state and are still feeling those final moments before they died, meaning that the pain and suffering hasn't left them at all. They are still living it. A basic level of respect should be considered here, and it's called human decency.

I often go into a location that has activity in order to find out what we are dealing with in that particular; location but only if the intention is pure and loving with the best intentions of resolution for both sides, the physical and metaphysical. They should not be here and, ultimately, assisting them in crossing over is the goal, regardless of a positive or negative someone, or multiple someone's, who may be present. They should be where they can be healed, loved and remember who they really are. If you are looking for drama, over-reacting and zero results then don't call me, go ahead and call the ghost busters, because I'm not available for any of that.

I must include in here negative or dark entities. Some people might call them demons. I am not bringing this subject up in order to frighten anyone, but to bring empowerment through knowledge.

The last thing I ever wish to do is to bring fear to anyone, in fact the total opposite is where the truth lies here. The last thing you should ever have is fear of any ghost, and that includes anything negative that might be hanging around, therefore, education is the key to overcoming this falsely created fear factor. Don't get me wrong, I too have experienced fear from ghosts of every type for a long number of years and, it began in my childhood where I had many ghostly encounters all the way into my adult years. Ultimately, it was knowledge and understanding that conquered it, and I overcame the situation. Therefore, I have a desire to bring education and understanding to others in order to eliminate this fear of what is unknown. Because negative entities do exist, and therefore, I do have to mention them in this chapter. They come from different places and, there are different levels to them so, let's explore that a little bit here.

There are ghosts that are not dark entities, or necessarily negative, but can be mean, angry or grouchy just because that was their personality in life, or because of the situation surrounding their exit, or because of the people who are now occupying their space, and so on. These are not dark entities, they are simply people who require assistance in crossing over in order to receive the healing and love they require, and the sooner the better. I mean who likes a grouchy ghost in the house anyway, right?

We have entities that were once human and became so distorted from negativity that they are no longer human. This happens completely by their own choice. I really would like to reiterate that this was their own choice and not due to any kind of punishment as we sometimes are led to believe. My daughter had just such a person occupying her house, and we didn't discover this until after the purchase was made. Yes, two psychics did not immediately catch this until after the move. My daughter, Kayla, was the first to discover him shortly after moving in, while I was away visiting a friend in Alamosa, Colorado. She called to tell me there was a tall dark entity that felt male in the dining room. This felt very negative and dark to her.

Regardless of whether you think you are psychic or not, everyone is capable of receiving this information, please trust this feeling and do not talk yourself out of it because that is what someone told you to do or because that is what you think you should do. If this is what you feel, then know you are accurate and always trust it. She had a few sparse run-ins with him while I was away, and this was all we knew of him in the beginning. I hadn't come across him but got a very strong knowing that he liked to travel the entire neighborhood which consisted of 97 houses all on five-acre lots. This quickly changed when my son got deployed to Qatar and his pregnant wife moved in with us, along with her two children, Emile, who was not yet two, and Izzy, who was five. They all three moved into our guest bedroom and immediately began to have experiences. Often, Christina came out of the room frightened and insisting someone was in the closet, yet every time we investigated, he already had left. This seemed to be a regular pattern of his. He began manipulating her dreams and every, morning at 3:00 a.m., Emile would wake up crying and shaking. At first, Christina thought it was his teething getting to him so the first few nights we didn't think much of it, but one morning after a few hours of it I offered to take him from her to give her a break. I brought him into my room where he immediately fell asleep from exhaustion. Then I had my first encounter with the tall dark guy in a large hat. He stood in my room looking right at me, and I knew immediately he was there for the baby. I said, "Oh no, you don't," and I immediately put up a golden light barrier around the bed. He was unable at that point to get to me or the baby. While I was able to create a sufficient barrier at the time, my barrier abilities at this juncture were nowhere near as powerful, or as knowledgeable, as they are now. This happened several nights in a row, and I quickly learned that he had become powerful in his time of occupying our third dimension after his untimely death. He would stand next to my bed and attempt to manipulate my thoughts in his attempts to get me to invite him across my barrier, so he could get at the baby. Absolutely not! He was never successful, but he tried.

Then one night I was headed for bed, after staying up late, and I saw him in the size of a dog as he crawled, or I should say more like scurried, through my window and hurried himself under my bed. Okay, I will play that game. I got into bed and put up a barrier around him trapping him there for the night. Lo and behold, Christina had no nightmares that night, and the baby slept all night without a hitch. Then, Christina decided to move into our office in order to get away from him. That night I had dreams of pretty much the only thing that creeps me out, a pile of snakes! Little did he know, I have been working with my own dreams for several years by now, and instead of being frightened, I acknowledged the dream and asked myself, "Why are you dreaming about snakes, and what does this mean?" At that very moment he had an, "Oh shit she knows I'm here," moment and I had an instant, "Oh he's under my bed manipulating my dreams," moment. This seemed to happen simultaneously. He booked it out through the window as I woke up before I could trap him again. He decided to make me his enemy after that, and from then on, he began following me all around the property as I did the chores and such outside, inside, wherever. He often traveled and looked like Gollum from Lord of the Rings except he was all black. Once, he tried to knock me off a step stool but wasn't strong enough to get it done, one time he scratched my back and once he jumped on me when I was in bed and began punching me furiously. It didn't hurt, but nonetheless he was attempting it. Time went on, and with zero interference this type of behavior will become strong enough to hurt. After a short time, he realized what room Emile had been moved to and resumed his attacking of the baby at 3:00 a.m. I banished him from the property because I had yet to learn how to completely remove him by sending him to source at this time. After his banishment, I often saw him standing across the street in the neighbor's front yard glaring at me in his tall dark-hat-wearing form. One day at a neighborhood gathering I casually asked, while sitting close to the neighbor whose house he was currently occupying, if anyone had any strange events that have occurred in the neighborhood. Of course, this neighbor, who had lived there for seventeen years and had six kids of varied ages, had very similar experiences as we have had with this guy. The entire time she has lived in the house, coincidentally, he literally was gaining his strength by picking on the children and feeding on fear. Her teenage daughters seemed quite relieved to finally have someone else who has experienced this, as their reaction in unison was, "See mom, we told you he's real." I told her how I banished him off my property and I could help her do the same. Her response was, "No I don't want to make him angry." Let me ask you something. Would you tolerate it if a grown man was coming into your home in the middle of the night and harassing your children in their sleep? Then don't tolerate this from somebody in ghostly form either! This is not okay, and you are responsible for keeping your kids safe! I understand if someone doesn't know how to deal with it, but I have zero tolerance for someone who would allow their kids to suffer so they don't have to face and conquer their own fear in order to protect their children.

Kayla and I decided to get to the bottom of this and find out who and what we are dealing with. So, with a psychic connection that Kayla did, we discovered that he came from the east coast, possibly New York and was traveling with a group of people through Oklahoma on their way to California. He somehow became separated and lost from his group and found himself in southeastern Colorado, all alone, when a group of Native Americans had discovered him. They spent three days torturing him, before finally killing him and leaving him there which, coincidentally, was just prairie land uninhabited by anyone except animals until this neighborhood had been developed in the late 90's. And, it just so happens that the exact location he died was right outside the window of our guest bedroom. He could have gone home with the Angels to be healed, but he consciously decided that he would stay to exact his revenge on those who did this to him. The problem is that the people who did this to him didn't live there and were now long gone leaving him to wait over 150 years for someone to show up so he could fulfill his determination in creating fear, pain and suffering among them. The result was him picking on babies, pregnant women and sick people.

Yes, I feel compassion for the man who had such a horrible exit when all he did was get lost, I don't feel sorry for the man who chose to not go home, picks on babies and allows his hate and revenge-driven ego to make him so distorted that he wasn't even human anymore. I did eventually learn how to send him back to source and relieve the entire neighborhood of him.

There are entities that people may call demons and there are different levels and types of them, as far as how dark they are and how strong they are, and what kind of jobs they have. Yes, like us light entities these guys have certain roles to play, and to the human understanding we would call it a job. But, please, be aware that nothing exists that is stronger than you are. You are a shining bright light of the creator with an overwhelming ability to flush out the darkness of any negative being. It's more or less a matter of knowing how. Also, please know, absolutely, there is no one all-powerful devil who is out to get you or steal your soul or do anything to lead you astray from the light and so forth. It was 100% made up by the church, and research into the history of it and where it originated, will quickly prove this to be true. Do your own research and don't take my word for it. Find the facts and know your history. However, there are a wide variety of lower level entities, and you can call them demons if you are more connected to this labeling of things, if you wish. It doesn't really make any difference anyway.

They are not human and never have been. They travel at a much lower frequency than we do, and this, is why they are dark and difficult to see with our own eyes. Often, they might be seen just like with positive entities out of the corner of your eye, yet when you turn to look no one, or nothing is there. This is because the dimensions break at a 45 degree angle and gives you a glimpse into this other dimension that they occupy. Pretty much any level of creep factor, or shape and figure, these beings can come in and they have. There are portals to these lower levels, and I am not certain at this point why, or how, they were all created except that there are man-made ones, I do know not all of them are created this way. I am not going into any detail as to how they make them, and I personally don't know the exact way to do it anyway, other than a general understanding. I am only aware of some of what would have to take place and it's quite disturbing. Let's just suffice it to say it is not possible with a Ouija board, which I am against using by the way. I may not know the exact way to open a portal, but I do know enough about what it entails to not desire a discussion for it here other than it is very dark stuff, and if that seems to be your interest then I am sorry to say you have picked up the wrong book

I would like to explain portals and gateways. There is a difference. My sister, Linda, did live next to a gateway that, literally was right outside her back door. These entities are the thickest near the entrance of a gateway, or portal, and that can and does mean many miles out, getting worse as you get closer to the exact location. Something to note right now is that there are many different types of portals and gateways, I am only referencing ones to the lower dimensions at this point. Now with a gateway once they emerge, they may come and go but generally staying fairly close to the entrance. Some of them can continue to wander farther out away from their original location, looking for an opportunity to cause a disturbance in your reality. This is more common than most people are aware.

Anyway, my sister and her boys suffered for years before I discovered this portal. Because they lived maybe a half-mile or so from it originally and moved to the house that was literally right in front of the portal years later, which is when it was discovered. At this time, it was my friend, Tami, who knew it was there and told me to look for it when I was discussing with her my sister's situation with this location and what I had already gotten from it. It sure does help to have more than one psychic look into things, because as we work together, we can get separate information that seems to fit together. It is like working on a jigsaw puzzle together. We each have different pieces that fit together nicely. While Linda and her two boys lived in the vicinity of this gate, these negative entities wreaked havoc on them for years. These entities cause things like feeling tired a lot, nightmares, depression, suicidal thoughts, fighting and all levels of drama and negativity, along with every kind of physical and mental health issue imaginable when living in such a location. At this point I did not know how to shut down a gateway or portal. While I do have more knowledge about it at this juncture in my life, I am not at liberty to go into great detail with this writing. For now, the only advice I have for you if you live near a portal, or gateway, is to move and the farther away the better. Do not take fear with you but just know that it is healthier to live in a location with high vibratory energy that makes you feel good. Please do not give in to despair or fear, but only realize that this location is not conducive to a healthy living environment and a more suitable one is required. If you suspect this is what you are dealing with, but are uncertain, then please contact an experienced professional psychic who can help you determine this. Just because a location has plenty of activity does not mean you live near a portal. Remember there are portals all over the planet and they are not all bad. First determine exactly what you are dealing with, and whether you even should move to a more peaceful environment, rather than clear out the one you are in before you get too stressed out or worried about what is going on. A professional who has experience with these matters is who you should call. Just because someone is psychic doesn't mean they do this type of work, or even prefer to do this type of work.

When I asked my guide in connection to my sister's gateway, and specifically the entities clustering in and around her house because of it, how long has it been there, her answer was, "Before time." Now we all know time doesn't really exist, nor is it linear, but when I questioned my sons guides on this subject matter for more clarification, this is what they had to say. "Most gateways on this planet are very ancient. It takes a lot to close a gateway. It takes ceremony, stones, artifacts and old magic. Each one is unique unto themselves and what it would take to close one is quite detailed. There are many of them all over the planet, from very small to very large. A gateway is a two-way door and entities can go both ways. These are as old as the Earth herself in many cases, or close to it. A portal is something that was opened. In order to open one would take a ceremony and a group of people who really know what they are doing with the intention of opening this portal. To close a portal requires a group of advanced people who equally know exactly what they are doing and to perform a ceremony, at minimum, equal to if not stronger than the energy that created it in the first place. The minimum is three very advanced psychics to take down a very small one.

I would like to make it very clear that you cannot open a gateway or a portal by playing with things like the Ouija board. While I absolutely do not promote playing with things that attract who knows who, I would like to reiterate that you are just attracting someone who you probably would prefer not to have hanging around you, but this is not going to open a portal.

Here we are at another subject that is taboo, and that would be entity attachments and possessions. Which are two different things by the way. Positive oriented entities do not attach to you. Loved ones who have crossed over are not afraid of losing you and will always know where to find you if they choose to make a visit. If they are a positive-oriented ghost, then they may attach themselves to a certain place or an object due to an emotional attachment, as far as my understanding goes. They are not necessarily tethered to it and are able to leave at any time they decide it is okay to do so. They really don't care to attach themselves to you because they have their own stuff they are dealing with, and tormenting you is not necessarily high on their agenda in most cases. I say most cases because one thing I have learned over the years is that absolutely nothing is impossible. As always there are many things that are unlikely and things that are extremely rare.

If you are living in a house with negative entities, or energy, then you should notice a profound feeling of release when you are away from home as if a ton of bricks just got lifted off your shoulders. If there seems to never be a release, or you moved, and you are still seeing a certain dark figure in your closet, room, or whatever, and your experiences continue to be the same or similar, then perhaps you do have an attachment. At this point get a professional who is experienced with entity attachments to help. Or, if you have never had activity in your home before, yet now there seems to be some odd things going on, it is possible you picked something up somewhere and brought it home. Forget Hollywood and the church, with their exorcism ways, because it is all fake and will not work. First, you should know there are different ways and reasons for getting attachments, as well as many, different ways to get rid of them. And yes, it is possible to get rid of each, and every one of them. I currently don't know every possible way one may attach to you because there are so many, and I do know a long list of them. I will share only a few of the more common ones I see here.

I would like to clarify the difference between entity attachments and an actual possession. An attachment will tether a cord to you so that no matter where you go, they are able to find you. Think of it like a leash that gives them the freedom to come and go and cause whatever destruction they wish in whatever other location they wish, and they will return to you whenever they decide. Therefore, when you move to another house, no matter how far away from the last one you go, this entity or entities will always follow you. Even if you go to a location that they are blocked from they may still follow you.

Example: I had a client who brought her sixteen-year-old daughter to me who has had the same entity attachment since she was six years old. She just went for a walk with her family around the neighborhood, like so many of the rest of us do, and her being psychic saw this negative entity who looked like a creepy little girl from a scary movie standing behind a tree. This entity decided she liked the little psychic girl better than the people she currently had been tormenting, who didn't really see her or hear her so well, it's not near as fun as it is to pick on someone who can hear and see what she is about. Finally, after so many years of her nonsense they came to me. Because I have so many barriers up in my house the attached entity was unable to come in, thus finding herself waiting on the sidewalk out front. This psychic client then found her attached cords and cut them. I was able to trap said entity and have her hauled off back to source. Then I taught her how to put up some protection around her, and her home, on a regular basis to keep anything, or anyone else, away who do not come with pure intentions. Attachments literally can show up from anywhere, not just a haunted house. It could be from just walking down the road and one finds you. It could be something followed you back from the dream realm. It could be that someone else doing dark stuff attached one to you. It could be that you invited one in by surrounding yourself with negative activities and people. It could be that you are suffering from depression and one just found you because your frequency is so low. The list goes on and on and on. Therefore everyone on the planet should be working towards keeping their vibrations higher and their home protected.

Entity possession occurs more often than you think. One, of if not the most common way, is that you invited it or them in. This is not as cut and dry as, "Hey, you come on over here and stay with me." If the world only began to see them so clearly, they would be shocked at what they saw running around and where. Let's talk about the most basic ones. These are almost never discovered and are easy to get rid of because it happens every day without most people even realizing it. When people get really drunk, especially when they black out or cannot remember anything, they really were possessed for that duration of time. Alcohol is not called spirits for no reason. This person checked out and another entity temporarily occupied their body. They literally gave their permission by using drugs or alcohol to the point that they chose to leave and allow somebody else to come along. Once the person passes out and wakes up sober, or partially sober, then it is no longer conducive for said entity to occupy their body any longer because they have raised their vibrations enough to be in their own body again. The other whomever was unable to stay due to unmatched frequency, as it is called.

Another way to get a temporary possession is to spend hours and hours on video games or zoned out scrolling on the phone or watching television. These people willingly check out of their bodies leaving themselves susceptible for an entity to temporarily take over. Once you get out of the zone and start living life again, they are unable to stay. In these situations, people are what you might call possessed, but once they choose to occupy their own self again there is no room for such low beings to stick around. The person did their own exorcism, you could call it, and kicked them out. The key here is to avoid such situations. No drugs, including too many prescriptions, no alcohol, limited electronics, and taking control of your own life. I know it is a lot of hard work, trust me I do know, but it is what's required.

Then we have the next level where people go looking for them, whether they know it or not. If you are starting to see dark shadows of people, or odd creatures where there wasn't any before, and you seem to be continuing to have experiences that seem new, then analyze what you have been doing lately to attract this. Are you playing with the Ouija board or similar games to attract literally anyone? And I don't mean Tarot cards or oracle cards because they don't do it. Are you listening to violent music or watching scary movies or reading scary books? Are you looking into dark magic or the negative side of paranormal events? Are you occupying your time with negative things? Have you decorated your room with black or skulls or anything dark in nature? Negative breeds negative and you will attract whatever you surround yourself with. Get out and change your ways and do it immediately. Send them out of your life before it gets much worse and becomes out of your control. This is another way for both entity attachments and possessions to take place. Usually the attachment comes first, or, perhaps that is all you will be able to muster with your dark activities. Often this can and does grow into something more.

I know a situation that I prefer not to name people or give too many details. One person was always clearing, meditating, putting barriers up and focusing on loving and forgiving everyone, even if in some cases it posed challenges. Nothing can get in, right? Someone who was supposed to be a friend who dabbled in dark stuff, became upset one day for minor reasons at friend number one and sent a nasty entity attachment in the dream realm and every night for weeks friend number one would wake up with horrible scratches all over the body. Then moods became off, and as much work that was done to fix it with regular routines to keep the energy on a positive note, and it became a struggle. Fortunately, it was discovered what was causing the trouble, where it came from and how to get rid of it. That entity has been successfully reabsorbed into source energy and will no longer create a problem for anyone else.

Sometimes entities didn't attach because someone sent them or because you invited them in. Perhaps you just moved into a location or visited a location, where a negative entity just found you and was able to attach to you. The more psychic or intuitive you are, the more likely they are to want to follow you around, especially psychic children. Or, perhaps an object with a negative attachment was purchased. Let me just say that this new trend of knowingly and willingly purchasing objects from the Internet that are supposedly haunted is a bad idea all the way around. I highly doubt if most of those items are even legitimate, and secondly, the ones that are could be a positive, or a negative entity, and either way you most likely are getting yourself into a headache that you really don't want and definitely don't need. There are any number of reasons as to why an entity would attach itself to an object, or someone else attached it there, and none of them are good, even if the person who attached is nice, the reason for the attachment is usually not. It could range anywhere from something super negative wanting and willing to do you and your family harm, to someone with deep emotional issues and could use a psychic therapist or just a grouchy soul who has no desire to not be grouchy. So just do yourself and those around you a favor and steer clear of such things. Not out of fear, but just out of common sense.

There is a way to become fully possessed, and not like the spirits that will shortly occupy the body due to drugs or alcohol, but I mean a true come on in I will step aside possession where you both, or even more, are occupying the same body. Please, let me reiterate that this is not very easy to do for the common person. And, it too cannot happen without the person's permission. This includes some very disturbing ceremonies and activity that I refuse to discuss here and, again, I will reiterate that if this is your interest you are absolutely reading the wrong book. All I am going to say is how it doesn't happen. It doesn't happen to your average everyday teenager going off to college who seemingly catches a cold and then comes home possessed! That is all in the movies and not reality. It doesn't tend to happen to regular everyday ordinary people minding their own business and just living their life. Even if they move into a house packed with negative beings, or even a portal to the lower dimensions, it just doesn't happen that way. It only happens to those who welcome them in and perform the right ceremonies. Then they often go on to live a glorified life of wealth and power in most cases. If someone is truly possessed by one of these entities, or possibly multiple entities, I understand the next question of concern is how to get rid of them. First, the person has to want to be rid of them, because they are the ones who invited them in. Second, this is very difficult because, most likely, the person you have, to talk to is in the background and the entity is in the foreground of who you are dealing with. I personally have never, not once, had to deal with this, so I am going to relay what was told to me by my guides on how to solve this problem. "The original soul has to order and demand they leave. They have, to leave once ordered to go. Darkness can't exist where there's light, so once this person connects to the light of origination (I believe this to mean the creator) the darkness won't want to stay. These dark entities are blocking out all contact and communication with Angels or guides." So, I asked, "How do we get in touch with said person then?" and they said, "Telepathically, or in the higher realms, because most of them spend the majority, of their time outside of their body anyway."

I then asked, "Is it possible to get rid of the dark ones this way." And they responded, "Yes," the easiest way is to connect in the higher realms and convince them to return to their body and demand their own body back."

Question: "Once they are back in their bodies, what can we do to assist this person?"

Answer: I was shown a vision of bright light jumping back into the body and dark entities jumping out as if knocked over by a bowling ball. Then I hear, "Immediately put up a light shield."

Question: "What if there's no one available to connect with this person in the higher realms?"

Answer: "Almost impossible."

Question: "You said 'almost impossible', so there is a way. What is it?"

Answer: "Connect with guides and guardians from the deepest realm and ask for assistance in removing lower-level entities and take them back to source."

Question: "Am I right in thinking that the original entity has to come back?

Answer: "They will be forced back with no other choice. But they might not like it. The greedy part of them that made them do it in the first place is still there, and most likely will do it again."

Question: "Am I right in thinking they require deep therapy?"

Answer: "Therapy only works on those who want it. These people are surrounded by their own kind who will never let this happen. Not for love of others, but for self-preservation. If you flush out one, you might flush out them as well."

Question: "What about when Jesus ordered the spirits out of the three possessed men and they then jumped into the three geese nearby that proceeded to jump off of a cliff and kill themselves?"

Answer: "Those were entity attachments, not possession, and once you know and understand your true power this would be easy to do."

So, basically, it doesn't look like I personally will come across such a situation where I am dealing with a true entity possession, and that's good. Not because I'm frightened, but because it doesn't seem like an easy task and chances are, most likely, they will go right back and do it again. How frustrating. This is really, as far as I'm willing to go on this subject matter in this book because I only wanted to touch base on it and eliminate most people's fear of entity possessions.

Now on to poltergeists! Poltergeist is a German word created sometime in the early 1900's from the word postern meaning to create a disturbance and Geist meaning ghost. This translates into ghosts that make a disturbance, such as knocking things over, banging, rattling or, in my niece's situation, her poltergeist squeezed the toothpaste out all over the dog when nobody was home, amongst other messes. No worries, I took care of him for her and he has gone back to the Other Side. Some ghosts can and will do these things, however, the majority, of them do not, and often, the culprit of such goings on is actually someone in the house. That's right, a family member, and often that family member is a child with psychic abilities. For instance, if this child or teen has been suppressing their abilities, or emotions, and simply do not know or understand how to direct this energy yet, then this can create a real problem. Undirected energy of this magnitude on a minor level could rattle or bang things in the house, while on a massive level could create what's called a thought form. And yes, these become real live dark entities that begin to create their own havoc, either on the person who created it or those nearby, even unsuspecting neighbors or guests or a new occupancy of the home. Just like any other lower dimensional being, you definitely would not like one of these attaching themselves to some unsuspecting someone and manipulating their life. (Just a note that this is not the only way thought forms are created.)

This is serious business as this is exactly the type of entity that attached to my nephew at age 11 and was successful in murdering him by age 22. This is the reason I dedicated so many years of my life to learn about dark entities and dark magic and all the deeply disturbing things that hurt and upset me so much. I found my strength, my power, my knowledge and my understanding of these things all the while shedding my fear, only to be about three weeks too late in learning how to trap such a being and send him back to source. This is one of the reasons I am sharing knowledge here. Because more knowledge out there will help to save, and/or protect, people from such an experience. How do we direct this energy before one of these guys shows up? Or even after one shows up? Doing yoga combined with either T'ai-Chi or Qigong on a regular basis is just one of the ways this energy can be directed. This is not to be stopped because the cupboards stopped rattling, but this is a life-long endeavor and a way to always direct and manage the energy. Much of what I know how to do today I have to attribute to the energy I learned from doing T'ai-Chi and Qigong. Also, figure out who in the house is doing this and begin meditation and mindfulness classes immediately. Now As for the thought form, he's easy. You can pour liquid silver light on him and dissolve him. Go into a meditative state, locate him wherever he is in the house and literally watch a thick silvery liquid pouring over him and dissolving him. If you are unable to do this then please contact a psychic who does this type of work to get rid of him. They should not even have to come to the house, they should be able to do it right there on the phone. He will immediately dissolve and be no more of a bother to you or anyone else.

So, this leads me to, "How we get rid of all these other disturbances?" In some cases, they really are not that simple, and a professional is required. On the other hand, in many cases, it really is possible to fix these things on your own. First off, avoid negative things or anything that might cause you to feel fear, whether real fear, or falsely created has no matter here just stay away from it always. It's a low-level vibration and it attracts such things as negative entities. And, while I understand that grief is a natural process, we all can experience when someone we love transitions to the other side, the road back to living life can be very difficult for many of us. Grief does go through stages and it's different for each person. There is no set standard on how it has to go. Grief is such a low vibratory emotion that it's very damaging to stay there any longer than necessary. I am truly not wanting to be uncaring in this discussion (my family has lost three of our children within a year's time), so I honestly do have the best of intensions discussing the emotion of grief. And, while not everyone experiencing grief has an entity attached to them, they are ripe for the picking, so to speak. Negative entities feed on energy as a food source, and emotions such as fear, grief, depression, and anxiety are just places they love to feast. While this stuff is in the air, they feed the most off the direct energy source the person providing that source.

All negative emotions offer a food source, so please be careful of your own emotions and how others feel in your presence. No, you are not responsible for someone else's emotions as we can only be responsible for our own, however, we can be responsible for our words and actions, as they do send both a positive and negative energy towards others. Stop feeding the negative entities on the planet, and you will be helping to do your part in reducing their food source.

Smudge your house daily with sage, or a Palo Santo stick. Most health food stores sell it, as well as metaphysical shops, some crystal shops, and it can be purchased online. First, open windows and/or doors in the home. The energy, even transmuted energy must have a place to go, and that place is out. When you light your sage, I recommend a shell, or plate, to hold under it in case a spark falls, but I have been smudging for 20 years and have not lit anything on fire yet. Pick a starting point in the home, and it can be anywhere, then walk clockwise around the house from room to room until you reach your starting point and continuously repeat the words. "I release all energy and entities into the white light of the Holy Spirit for purification." You now have cleansed your house out. Then turn and go counter, clockwise repeating, "Only joy, love, wonder, inspiration, gratitude and prosperity will thrive in this home." Until you again reach your starting point. You have now replaced all negativity in the home with positive energy. This should be done every day and I don't care if you have ghosts or not, this is necessary to raise the vibrations of the home and keep your space purified. This also will set up a barrier to repel negative stuff from coming inside. It is important to know that it does wear off, so if you fail to keep up on it then this will stop working. You also might discover that the negative people in your life will stop coming over. They will not really know exactly why, but they will be very uncomfortable in your house, as will pesky people you don't know knocking on your door. They will just avoid it and they don't know why. Negativity comes in all forms, so just repel that stuff right out. Failing to smudge your house regularly is like failing to dust it regularly and the dirt gets built up. You even bring it in yourself, and this goes for every person and home on the planet. Because every time we have a negative feeling or thought, or an argument with someone, or guests over, or even left the house to the store and came back, we bring that stuff right back in so transmute it and send it out. And don't forget to do under the beds and in the closets. Energy definitely gets stagnant in those locations. This can also be done to any outbuildings such as the garage, shop, shed, barn, etcetera. Burning incense is an energy cleanser too, however, it is not at strong.

Another protective barrier that can be put up is to be done every morning before you even get out of bed. Picture a golden energy encompassing you and say, "I only allow into my energy field that which serves my highest good. I allow nothing into my energy field that hinders me from following my Divine purpose." Negative people will have no idea why, but they will tend to avoid you. The instant you decide to feed into negativity, say something negative to someone, or take part in unnecessary drama or participate in any form to that which does not serve your higher good this shield will have been distorted due to you taking it down, so it is important to be conscious of your actions and words.

How did I trap that negative entity under the bed and keep him from influencing my dreams all night? Simple. I surrounded him under there with a golden light and asked all of my guides and Angels to surround him and hold him until the sun came up. I slept wonderful, which has always been difficult for me, and then I awoke right as the sun was coming up only to discover he and my Angels were gone. Another way to keep negative entities from being under the bed, is to put a black Obsidian pyramid under each corner of the bed. If you are unable to buy four at once, a single, one under the center is enough until you are able to obtain all four.

One thing that is really, important for you to remember is that you are a powerful light being, and there is nothing from a lower dimension that is stronger than you are. Also, remember that these techniques are by no means all there is to eliminate negative entities, not even close, but this is a good place to start and build up your knowledge from there. But, remember, that even if you smudge, put up your light shields and have every bed in the house protected from underneath. This is really, only good for negative entities. If you have a positive ghost in the house this will not send them outside, not even if they are grouchy positive ghosts. If you have done the things I already listed, and your situation has not changed, then please get help from someone who specializes in this situation before you spend more money. Please ask first if they do this exact type of thing, not just sage and leave, because I just taught you how to do that for yourself.

Also, please remember this situation requires love, guidance, and compassion not fear and drama. Most ghosts are not necessarily dark entities, even if they are full of negative energy, because, generally, they just have issues that require some level of counseling and, let's face it, so do most of us on this planet. They just require some love and guidance in order to cross over, and personally, I feel that this is the only compassionate and humanitarian thing to do. Think about if this ghost was one of your loved ones, wouldn't you prefer that someone help them to cross over where they will receive the love and healing, they deserve?

When a soul enters a new body while in the womb people believe this to be a beautiful and loving thing to happen. We rejoice over it. Yet when a soul is finished with their experience here, and they exit that same body, regardless of their age, we develop fear of that exact same soul whom we were excited to have enter this reality. Now does this seem logical to you? Not only is it illogical, it is downright distorted. The truth is that we have no need to fear entities, positive or negative, we should try only to understand who they are and who we are and, more precisely, who you are. For we are all spiritual beings having a human experience, not humans hoping to someday have a spiritual experience. Our spiritual experience is ongoing and it includes this human existence as only a small part of it while, simultaneously, we share this experience with many other entities from many other dimensions and levels of advancement. We are all connected as one through our infinite creator. And, in that, there is no room for fear, only love and light for all.

CHAPTER SIX

UNDERSTANDING ENERGY

Energy healing? What is that? I am an energy healer for people, dogs and horses, yet I often get asked what is that? With an awkward look. People don't really have to tell me what they are thinking because I'm an empath and I already know how they feel about it. I'm pretty sure it does not require empathic abilities to figure it out. They think I am crazy, or just "don't believe in that stuff." It took a long time for people to accept the benefits of chiropractic care, message therapy, or acupuncture, which is a form of energy healing by the way; therefore, I understand that this is a new concept and so many people have never heard of it, or they just don't understand or trust it at this juncture. This is the healing of the future. With names like Reiki and healing touch, society is slowly, yet surely becoming more familiar and comfortable with the idea of energy healing. However, energy healing does not require a name. These are only names of different techniques for doing the same thing.

There is a medicine free-energy healing hospital in China called Chi-Lel founded by *Dr. Pang Ming* that uses only energy to heal people, yet they boast healings such as an elderly woman being cured of bladder cancer. This was well documented by *Luke Chan* who wrote about it in his book, *"101 Miracles of Natural Healing."* This hospital does have equipment such as an EKG, CT, X-ray and ultra-sound machines. It also keeps a staff of over 600 to include at least 24 doctors trained in Western medicine who are in charge of diagnosis on intake, and upon release, as well as regular checkups. The hospital relies on three major fundamental understandings on healing.

Everyone is called student and not patient, no matter how sick the person is. This terminology makes perfect sense to anyone who has even a little bit of understanding of energy and how powerful our words can be that affects this energy field. Patient implies sick, which only creates illness within the energy field, while student is very accurate as a student of energy, which we all are whether we know it or not. So rather than a doctor/patient relationship it becomes a teacher/student relationship as the student begins to learn self-healing through energy. As an energy healer myself, I can assure you that I am not doing my job properly if I am not encouraging every client, I see to do their own energy work resulting in visiting me on a less frequent basis. People might think this is not good for business, however, if I betray the universe by putting myself ahead of educating people that they can manage most if not all their energy themselves, I assure you I will stop getting clients altogether. And, besides, when people understand their own energy they will know when they require a visit to me while managing themselves in-between. Even us energy healers visit each other on occasion.

Focus on energy gathering and learning how to utilize the energy gathered. This second understanding teaches the students how to take charge of their own energy by filling their days up to a full eight hours of learning how to cultivate the life force energy, and the transformation of matter into energy, and vice versa. Ultimately, this is what learning to understand the energy is all about.

Focus on love or oneness. This helps the students focus on the understanding of their own power and abilities through love, which is the most powerful of energies. In a group they learn to offer support and love to one another, while creating a healing environment called the Qi (chi) field (chi means energy). This seems to have been proven effective by Russian scientific research. They have proven that phenomena such as clairvoyance, intuition, self-healing, and affirmations have a positive influence on the auras around people, and that words really do influence our DNA to include healing on a cellular level. They discovered that our DNA not only is responsible for the construction of our bodies, but it also is an informational data bank. The Russian biophysicist and molecular biologist *Pjotr Garjajev*, along with his colleagues, discovered that the human chromosomes function just like holographic computers. They managed to modulate certain frequency patterns, using a laser ray, and with it influenced the DNA frequency, thus the genetic information itself. They proved that one can simply use words and phrases from the human language! This explains why things such as affirmations, hypnosis and the like, have such a strong effect on the human psyche and the physical body. Esoteric and spiritual teachers have known for thousands of years that our body and minds are programmable through language, words and thoughts. This has now been scientifically proven to be true and this hospital in China, who didn't require Russia to prove it, is already using this as part of their healing program

But, with a world that is so sold on taking a pill for everything and convinced surgery is the only way, how can energy healing really take off? Simple. The energy will spread within the human consciousness. It is inevitable, because once it has entered the human consciousness grid it will spread throughout humanity. Science has proven that to be an inevitable fact as well, due to the fact that the human consciousness is intertwined with our physical reality.

Nikola Tesla said, "The day science begins to study the non-physical phenomena, it will make more progress in one decade than in all the previous centuries of its existence. To understand the true nature of the universe, one must think in terms of energy, frequency and vibration." You see, as more and more people begin to understand the idea of energy as healing, it literally becomes shared within the human consciousness and people are affecting other people whom they never even met. There is an energy grid that surrounds the planet, not only that but each species be it plant, reptile, insect, animal or human, each have their own energy grid distinct to that species. The science suggests that once a knowledge of, well anything reaches a critical mass then it will explode and seem to reach everyone in an "aha" moment. This may seem slow in the beginning, until this critical mass has been reached, but once it gets there it will advance at an incredibly fast rate throughout the human psyche.

This is commonly referred to as the hundred-monkey effect based on a study done in the 1950's of wild Japanese monkeys. As it turned out, these monkeys seemed to like sweet potatoes, unfortunately, they didn't care much for the sand or dirt upon them. One day a young female monkey figured out how to wash her potatoes and shared this idea with some of her playmates. As time went on over the years of study, more and more young monkeys began to wash the potatoes and even teaching their own parents how to wash them, while the older males who had little interaction with the youngsters had not quite gotten the concept. Then, at one point, a certain number of monkeys figured out the washing technique and the idea seemed to have expanded to most of, if not all, of the monkeys possibly in only a day. This story has become quite popular in describing how the morphogenetic field works and even leading to studies being done on humans. But, what does this story really say about morphogenetic fields? Possibly not much, but the story does break it down into a basic understanding that is quite easy for pretty much everyone to understand the concept of how the consciousness of the field spreads, which I believe is why it has become so popular.

As this understanding progresses throughout the human consciousness, and it will, only then we will begin to see energy healing become a more accepted and commonly understood idea. Healing will then become less invasive with zero narcotics, and the easier-on-the-wallet healing of our future. The most exciting thing about it is that it has already begun, so we don't really have to wait for it.

How does this work exactly? The more people who change their frequency is helping others to change their frequency. What is frequency? it is the rate at which atoms and sub-particles of a being travels or vibrates, so to speak. This vibrational frequency is true for everything in creation be it human, animal, fish, plant even water or air, or an entire planet. Everything in the universe is energy and energy vibrates. This is your frequency, as well as everyone and everything else, to include an entire universe even.

Because we are all vibrational energy, which is frequency, it only makes sense that we are, able to heal our bodies through sound. Frequency literally damages the human body as well as heal the human body. *Dr. Masaru Emoto* did an experiment where he froze water, and then looked at it under a microscope. On all of the water he played classical music to, or wrote the words, "I love you," prayed over it, or showed it positive pictures to then proceed to form the most amazing and beautiful crystal patterns. Yet, on the water they played angry music, did not pray over, wrote, "I hate you and I want to kill you," on it or showed disturbing pictures to it, then froze the water, it came out looking brown, cloudy and distorted under the microscope. The human body is made up of 60% water, while the brain and heart are both made up of 73% water, and the lungs are made up of 83% water. If these disturbing words, images, and sound frequencies we call music have this much impact on water, then how much do these things impact the human body? When these distortions take place, it does begin to manifest into physical and emotional symptoms. This experiment showed us that non-resonating vibration can result in destructive, energy and nothing can be created out of it except illness.

Given this experiment, I do believe it is safe to say that sound frequency has a huge impact on not only the human body, but everything in creation. In the realm of healing techniques, sound healing seems to still be so foreign to the Western world, yet it has been used successfully for thousands upon thousands of years. Much of, yet not all of, the current idea of sound healing stems from the work of researcher *Gerald Oster* during the 1970's who showed that when music is played in one ear and a different sound is played in another ear, the brain itself creates an entirely different sound called a binaural beat. This syncs the brain waves in both hemispheres creating a process called brain wave entrainment, which creates a pattern for healing.

This sound healing on a cellular level can also be created with tuning forks. A tuning fork proves useful in showing us how an object produces sound, and this also is true for the physical body. The tuning fork vibrates when hit against a rubber mallet, yet when it gets to an energy blockage in the human body it will instantly stop vibrating. This is an indication that the energy healer should give this area extra attention. These various types of tuning forks also can send a vibrational sound through the human body creating healing within that body structure. This also can be achieved at varied levels through devices such as Tibetan singing bowls, gongs, and humming. The wondrous results of the tuning forks are something I have witnessed first-hand-healing happen within only a few minutes of use, as well as with the Tibetan singing bowls and gongs in healing individuals from stress, chronic pain, depression, and even some forms of disease.

Let's discover why this is really so. We already know that the entirety of creation is sound frequency, therefore our own frequencies become distorted through various negative sound vibrations, to include visual and physical. Physics is now proving through quantum entanglement that all life was created through one source, therefore, we are all connected through this energetic force as well. As energy expands, the information expands and begins to take up more and more space as this expansion takes place. Does this not then make sense that when negative words are spoken to us, even to include the negative words we speak to ourselves or others, would have an impact on our energy field creating this energetic block that causes the illness we so desperately seek medication to hide? We do not seek medication to cure anything, we seek medication to hide the symptoms of the problem. Yet we so often tend to do nothing to clear the energetic distortion that is creating the issue. We all have three bodies: the physical body, the spiritual or soul body, and the energetic body. If even one of these bodies gets distorted, or ill, in any way it effects the other two. The health of all three should be equally important and not just the physical symptoms of a problem in the physical body while the others are completely neglected.

This is not just spiritual mumbo jumbo either, according to what is called epigenetics and the work of *Dr. Bruce Lipton*, and other researchers, our thoughts and impressions have been proven to have a direct impact on our DNA. The idea that we are completely powerless over our own body, and even the world around us, is complete nonsense. Scientists have completely shattered this dogmatic idea proving that we all have a great deal of control over our own genetics. This was mainly discovered from *The Human Genome Project* that was launched in 1990 and finally completed in 2003.

Along with this, the British molecular biologist *John Cairns* in 1988 presented his evidence that our responses to the environment in which we live affect our genes. This was a very shocking new idea, to be sure in today's world let alone 30 years ago.

You see, we are energy and energy is information, therefore, the energy within the body be it positive or negative, is storing information and continuously releasing it within the body. As we change our own thought processes about the energy, our words and what we expose ourselves to, we are literally changing our own biology. We are also affecting the way our nerves and neurons are interacting with each other, and this goes far beyond our human bodies. We are then even changing the world around us by changing the vibratory pattern we are in.

This goes into *Newton's* laws of energy and the motion of energy. It is the motion of this energy that we are directing through our lives and through our bodies. The first law is the law of motion. This law states that a body at rest stays at rest, while a body in motion stays in motion until something interferes with it. Everything about your life is in motion; relationships, careers, habits, whatever, and this even include the internal energy of the body. Energies that flow, both external and internal be it positive or negative, will stay the same until something interferes with it. This is where an energy healer comes into play. We break up that stagnant energy giving it increased positive flow allowing the healing process to begin. This is to include both physical and emotional. Therefore, we are the force that interferes with it. Then it becomes positive energy flowing in a fluid and healthy pattern, until something interferes with it yet again, whether positive or negative. Regardless, it does take intervention to direct the flow of energy.

While there are several laws that Newton put forth, we will only be examining the main three today, the second one is, "The force acting upon an object is equal to the mass of that object times it's acceleration." The bigger the energy it is we would like to change, the more force it is going to take to change it. If you have a constant habit of saying negative things like, "You're breaking me," guess what? Your body is literally going to begin to breakdown, and you are creating this energy to happen. Or, perhaps, there was a major trauma in your life that was never dealt with. That energy distortion creates a huge energy block that is causing pain inside the body. It is going to take a lot of energy work to break up and change these things.

The third Law is, "For every action, there is an equal and opposite reaction." What we put out, and how strong we put it out is exactly how it comes back to us. This includes words, thoughts, intentions, and actions. What comes around goes around. Truer words have never been said. So be careful exactly what you are sending out because that stuff absolutely, without a doubt, comes right back to you. Even if someone does something to hurt or offend or upset you in anyway, by sending a negative word or thought or action in their direction, it absolutely has to come back to you. So just let the universe take care of whoever it is that hurt you and walk away or as difficult as this may be, send intentions of love in their direction and this will come back to you in many ways.

When we distort our own selves, or allow another to do so, we create our own physical illness. This also means we have the ability to fix our own illness as well. Creating a healthy energy flow and learning to control it is what creates the healing. Taking control of your own energy will not only heal and empower you, but it will also create a world of wonderful things happening to and around you. We all are required to do more than just think about our energy fields even though this is a good place to start. And, there is no doubt that by changing the thought process other changes will begin to take place. But we are required to actively begin the change of the energy that acts upon us. At this point, we will find the healing because that is when we change the energy that acts upon itself. I am living proof of the effects this has on PTSD, depression, and anxiety.

We are conditioned to think that everything in the natural world is out of our control, yet it is actually the complete opposite. It is entirely in our control. We only have-to become students of the energy/Qi and realize that we are the energy. Your affirmation when doing the energy work like T'ai-Chi is, "I am the energy, it flows through me and from me."

As already stated earlier when we spoke about the Aura, everyone and everything has an Aura. Our Aura is our energy field that surrounds us and flows through us. It binds us all together throughout the universe, in this lifetime and all lifetimes to include our connections to the Other Side. This is the life force energy that requires our attention and healing because it affects everything within our bodies. I cannot express enough how important it is to conduct energy healing on a regular basis. This includes the balance and the flow of this life force energy. In order to accomplish this, I highly recommend an energy healer in your area to get you started and someone to visit on an as-needed basis. Provided you are staying on top of doing your own energy work, how often you require an energy healer will completely dependent upon the individual.

If this is not possible for you, there are many experienced energy healers that also do remote healing, meaning that they are able to work on you from wherever they are located. Traveling for either party is not necessary. I am available for this type of work as are many other healers I know that I'd be happy to refer. However, locating an energy healer in your area to work with when necessary is ideal but not necessary.

Also begin a regular yoga practice, and not this crazy Western fad yoga like power yoga, naked yoga, beer drinking yoga, or chicken nugget yoga. Yes, I have seen all, of this yoga, and it is not true authentic yoga. It is a disgrace to the practice of yoga. Please get into a true and authentic yoga program on some level of regularity. Ideally, it would be daily but, hey, start with whatever works for now, just as long, as you get started. Also, get into either T'ai-Chi or Qigong and make it regular as well. Again, ideal is daily but just start wherever you can right now. Gaia T.V. has plenty of authentic yoga and T'ai-Chi as well as Qigong. It can also be found on YouTube, DVD, and local classes. Many opportunities are available to incorporate this into your life.

This is only part of the regular energy work to be done because regular meditation practices and chakra balancing are equally important. These can be found in all, of the same places I mentioned above for the yoga. I personally meditate daily. An hour a day is recommended, but even fifteen minutes a day is better than nothing. I will admit that due to having my grandson on a daily basis, and he is only three years old, my meditation practice is quite challenged. I also balance my own chakras once a week but there was a time it was necessary for me to do this daily because they were such a hot mess.

What exactly are you doing by incorporating these practices into your life? You will be breaking up your own energy blockages and gathering energy and storing it up. This will give you increased energy levels, improved sleep patterns, as well as, the release of stress and past traumas. Also, you are activating and balancing your energy centers known as dantians and the chakras. This is important because as these energy centers shut down due to stress, trauma, and lack of bodily care, they can cause many health issues. *Dr Laura*, the intuition physician, has videos on YouTube explaining this. She is a Western-educated medical physician and she does understand the chakras play a key-role in our overall physical health. The chakras and dantians are energy vortex centers that are different from one another. However, they do act in conjunction with each other, therefore they are all important to understand. If getting healthy and staying healthy is your goal, please take into serious consideration the fact that your energy field requires you to heal it and keep it healed. Do not underestimate the effects the foods we eat have on our energy fields. Highly processed foods have little nutritional value, while foods that are closer to their original state, such as fresh fruits and vegetables, have a greater amount of nutrition, not only causing us to not be as hungry due to our nutritional needs being met, but it also helps with our energy fields and raising our vibrations. High vibratory food creates high vibratory energy within the body.

You are frequency. Frequency is sound. Sound is music. We are all music and we all travel at a vibration that is unique only unto ourselves. Yes, we make our own music and we are music. The Aura is made up of color. Color and sound vibrate together, or, should I say, as one and the same. Color/sound frequency makes up who we are. And what is color? Light! All, of the colors combined creates the light. Therefore, you are a powerful light being with your own unique sound frequency that plays your own music as you travel through not just this reality but all realities. Find your light being power because it comes from within you, not from some random outside source. And use this amazing light power to not just change your own DNA, but to change and alter the reality around which you exist.

When you awaken every morning before you even get out of bed, say to the universe, "Today I only allow within my energy field that which serves my highest good." By doing this one seemingly simple affirmation you are changing your frequency and what you are willing to allow within that frequency. If it does not serve your highest good, then it is not to come into your energy field. This includes negative people, actions, situations-everything. Take your bright light being self that you are and go out there and change the world you are experiencing!

CHAPTER SEVEN

UNDERSTANDING DREAMS

Dreams now here is a never-ending, and quite perplexing subject matter that has eternally intrigued the consciousness of man. So much so that every civilization, both modern and ancient, every religion and spiritual text, have all written upon this subject with great wonder, joy, intrigue and concern. They have made life changing decisions, as well as world changing, created wars, ended wars, changed diplomacy, religions, even science. Yet, still so many people comment, "It's just a dream, it's nothing." It's enough to make one very confused as to whether dreams are to be taken serious enough to make a drastic life change, or just write it off as nothing but the chaos of the mind during the sleep state.

Let's face it, we have all had dreams that have made us wonder what does it mean exactly, or does it even have meaning? Dreams surely have a way of leaving us quite perplexed as to their meaning, as well as if we should even take them seriously, or just go about our daily lives writing them off and never really getting to the bottom of them. Most likely many of you are resigning yourselves to the fact that we never will get the meaning of our dreams. Yet, there are many people who refuse to resign themselves to never having any answers to this, most interesting phenomena, choosing rather to spend a large portion of their lifetime trying to understand the dream realm. There are labs, machines, hospitals, and experts working daily to unravel the mysteries of the dream world. Why do we invest so much time, resources and investment into understanding our dreams if they are of no significance? The answer is simple they are significant, and they should be taken seriously. Humans are not the only ones who dream, much to the surprise of many. Studies have proven that animals, reptiles, birds, and even fish have dreams.

In order for us to understand the dreamworld we must first understand one thing; more reality happens during the dream state than in our waking hours. So, what is a dream anyway, and how do we understand these seemingly crazy experiences that make zero sense in our waking reality? Dreams are direct connections to our spiritual selves, therefore, I felt compelled to include a chapter on this very important subject. Let us explore the dream world as another aspect of our spiritual selves.

Our dreams provide us with an infinity of spiritual knowledge and putting forth some effort to decipher them is well worth our time as another way to advance our spiritual understanding of the self. More so than anything else when it comes to understanding our dreams, I recommend dream journaling. I personally always have a journal and pen right next to my bed to write down, immediately upon waking, whatever it is I remember, even if it is incomplete.

I am sure you likely have heard of someone, or even perhaps yourself, who have said, "I don't dream." The truth is, yes, you do. Everyone dreams, and it has been scientifically proven to be true. Just because you don't remember dreaming, doesn't mean that you don't do it. If you don't remember your dreams then perhaps just write down a feeling, or a knowing of something, if this happens to be so upon awakening. You also may ask your Angels to assist you in remembering your dreams before you go to sleep every night. Meditations before bed sometimes help with not only falling asleep and having a better night's sleep, but it could help remember dreams.

Before understanding the dream state, one must first understand the different stages of the sleep state as well as when we dream. There are four stages of sleep. The first stage is within the first ten minutes of sleep. This is a very light sleep stage and you can quickly and easily return to full consciousness if startled. This stage is so light that you may not even realize that you were even sleeping. When someone says were you sleeping? And you say something like, "No just resting my eyes, but I'm awake," this is in reality the first stage of sleep. Stage two of sleep generally happens about 10-20 minutes after falling asleep. This is where the heart rate slows and the body temperature drops. This is still considered a light sleep stage, although it may take some effort to awaken the person sleeping. Stage three sleep settles in about 35-45 minutes after falling asleep. And at this stage people are generally immune to the same noises that would awaken a person in the first or second stages of sleep. If you are awakened during this third stage of sleep, most likely you will feel disoriented for anywhere from a few, to even several minutes after waking. Until you adjust back to your waking self. The fourth stage of sleep is the deepest sleep and usually starts about 90 minutes after falling asleep. This stage is called R.E.M, rapid eye movement, because just as the name suggests your eyes rapidly move in all directions during this stage of sleep.

As the night progresses, these sleep cycles continue in a pattern with the dreamer moving in and out of the different stages of sleep. The R.E.M. stage of sleep is when all dreaming occurs, therefore, if you reach the R.E.M. state you most definitely have been dreaming. While in this state the body is completely paralyzed yet the brain functions as if you are fully awake and leading a very active life. Curious isn't it? Our minds are in full active mode while our bodies are literally paralyzed and seemingly unconscious.

All throughout history dreams have been believed to predict the future, resolve issues, bring spiritual understanding, and even cure illness. *Edgar Casey* was known as the sleeping prophet because he would enter into a dream like state in order to answer the questions of thousands of people across the country, and even the world who sent him letters asking for answers to everything from personal decisions to medical answers.

The earliest known records of dream journaling in our current history dates to around 3000 B.C. and includes dreams of both the Assyrians and the Babylonians. There are even clay tablets written in cuneiform, the oldest known written language, that speaks of

Gilgamesh, a warrior king of ancient Sumer, and how his mother, the goddess Ninsun, interprets his dreams. This is the oldest dream interpretation on known written record. I believe it would be safe to say this is not the first ever dream interpretation. This recording lends credit to the idea that humans have been interpreting dreams probably since we could communicate them.

The ancient Egyptians believed that we travel through a portal and into another dimension during our sleeping hours and that mystery dimension is where our dreams really come from. Dreams were so important to the ancient Egyptians that interpretation was commonplace among their daily lives. Around 700 B.C. in ancient Greece even Homer writes of dreams and their interpretations. And, in the second century A.D., the Romans began to catalogue and classify dreams. The Roman Artemidorus catalogued well over 3,000 dreams which is still considered today to be the first dream dictionary.

In India the Atharva Veda, which translates into "the procedures for everyday life" contains details of dreams to include how and why they occur, their purpose and how to interpret them. While in the Far East, both Taoism and Buddhism, teach that the worlds we see in our dreams are the worlds we will see after we leave this lifetime. In Celtic history, the Druids would interpret dreams where they would be incubated in tree groves and the spirits of the trees would be asked for assistance in these interpretations. During the Middle Ages, the Catholic church proclaimed that during dream time we are susceptible to the influence of the devil and to avoid his temptations of engaging in sin while dreaming. Therefore, dreaming was discouraged and those who had lucid or vivid dreams were accused of witchcraft or sorcery and could be killed for it. This put a quick end to dream interpretation in the Western part of the world for quite some time. Everyone was afraid to mention their dreams, and is it any wonder? Thank goodness burning at the stake for having a dream has ended. We can all sleep much easier now.

While the Western Europeans were surpassing their dreams,

the Aborigines of Australia live in what they call the Dreamtime. Dreamtime is a story of their history and how they came to be, their spiritual understanding of things, and everything brought forth around them came from the dream. They understand time is not linear, but everything is in a perpetual now. With this understanding they don't really differentiate waking hours with sleeping/dreaming hours, to them it is all the same. This understanding is shared with some African tribes as well, while others believe dreams provide wisdom from ancestors to assist them in daily life and decision-making which is why they incorporate their dreams into everything they do.

The Native Americans take on a similar understanding of our waking hours and dreaming hours, having no clear definition between the two. While each individual tribe tends to have their own understanding of dreams, they do seem to agree on the same understanding that dreams have the ability, to connect us with our deepest and truest spiritual selves.

With so many cultures that span the globe for thousands of years finding a value in understanding our dreams, it's quite understandable that it continues today with you, me and almost everyone else on the planet. And, while our understanding and ideas may still vary into the modern age, knowing what our ancestors thought of their dreams helps us to better understand our own dream world. Honestly, minus the devil influencing our dreams, and we should be burned at the stake or tortured in a dungeon beneath the church for lucid dreaming, I do respect all of the above ideas and I'm quite certain that they each have a level of accuracy we all can take into consideration when learning to better understand our dream world.

How do we decipher our own dreams without calling a dream interpreter every week? As I mentioned above, you should always keep a dream journal and pen next to your bed and record everything you remember about every dream, even if it is only part of the dream, to include seemingly unimportant and simple stuff. Also, note that the human brain will only remember, the dreams that were present within five minutes of waking up. That means we have many dreams throughout the night we don't remember, and this goes for all of us. Also write down your dream immediately, because within ten minutes of waking up you lose 50% of your memory of the dream and 90% within twenty minutes.

Next, categorize the dream. Once I learned the different categories of dreams, I was able to understand a great deal more of my dreams right away without help. Below I will include the different types of dreams for your interpretations. Write down which category your dream falls under, then you can move onto interpretation of said dreams.

Lucid dreams: Lucid means coherent or made aware of. These dreams also can be called a vivid dream. It simply means you become aware you are dreaming at any point during the dream itself. I often have lucid dreams and while my son, among many other people, prefer to take control of their dreams once they become aware that they are, actually dreaming, I personally prefer to watch and observe in order to take a mental note and write it down later when I am awake for deciphering. So yes, once you become lucid of your dream you are capable, with some practice, to direct and control your dream that you are aware of. Often, I will attempt to decipher the dream as I am watching it unfold. There is no right or wrong way between the two, just do whatever you prefer and that is perfectly alright.

Vivid Dreams: The slight difference between lucid and vivid would be that vivid dreams seem so real that it is difficult to decipher the difference between the dream and being awake in our current reality. It even may take several minutes to adjust to being back in this reality after waking from such a dream. Both lucid and vivid dreams are a high level of awareness and can happen with any of the following dream categories.

Astral Travel: Astral travel or astral projection is also commonly known as an out of body experience. Yes, you really do leave your body and astral travel to the Other Side, the inner realms, dimensions, timelines, and other locations to include both this lifetime, as well as others. You can even travel to the moon, or other planets, if you desire to do so. I astral travelled to another planet once and I specifically recall passing some sort of shuttle, or spaceship type craft, with two pilots that looked very close to humans here on earth before entering the planet's atmosphere. The two pilots were fully aware of me and clearly caught by surprise because they both looked right at me with a very shocked look on their faces. As I approached the planet, I had a familiar feeling of knowing this place, then as I flew over some rocky uninhabited small islands amidst hurricane type weather I knew exactly where I was! And I knew there was a large continent to my left, and I knew exactly where I was headed on that landmass! Then all-of-a-sudden, BAM! I was pulled back into my body. Was it just a dream? Absolutely, but we live full active lives during these dreams and the reality of our dreams is more real than the reality of our waking hours, so yes, this was real, and yes, this was just a dream. I know for a fact that you and/or someone you know has had a flying dream or a falling dream that cause the body to literally thump on the bed as you/they "land." That feeling of falling followed by your body thumping up off the bed as it jerks you awake is basically a crash landing back into your body after you have been traveling around. Let's just say it was less than a smooth return, causing such action.

I would like to address a notion that we shouldn't leave our bodies because it leaves us vulnerable for someone else to enter and occupy that body while we are away in our travels. Every human goes astral travelling every night as most R.E.M. sleep is astral traveling so there is no way to stop it. Let's examine the risk of becoming possessed. I'm sure in a Hollywood portrayal of possession is what usually comes to mind, wouldn't everyone on the planet already be possessed by now? Yes, you can, and many people do often bring back attachments, or I call them hitchhikers, but there is a simple way of avoiding this. Every night before you go to sleep you say, "Tonight when I journey into the sleep realm, I will only allow into my energy field that which serves my highest good, and beings who follow the one true law; the will to do good." This will avoid any hitchhikers from following you back in case you do end up traveling to a lower dimension. Nothing can attach to you and come back with you. This affirmation is a simple way to avoid this. Not being able to return to your body should never be a concern either because we are attached by a silver cord and most people see this cord at some point while traveling. Astral traveling doesn't always mean grand adventures either. Sometimes we just choose to fly around the neighborhood, or even just our house or visit friends or relatives' houses. We really have no boundaries, or even rules, when astral traveling and that I think is the most exciting part.

Sleep Catalepsy: This is not a dream category, so to speak, but I feel it is very important to include here for a few reasons. First, most people think they might be dreaming when this happens and, second, it is so terrifying at times that often people think they died, or became paralyzed, or are being attacked by evil forces. This happens when we are sleeping, and it can be quite frightening. I used to experience this often when I was a teenager, and I truly wish someone explained it to me because I experienced tremendous fear with this, and more than anything, I would like people to know that this is not to be feared. Sleep catalepsy is when you seem to be fully conscious, yet the body is completely paralyzed and unable to move or scream out for help. Some people even feel as though a dark entity is present or even sitting on top of them, possibly holding them down. And, yes, they probably are if this is what you are feeling during catalepsy. But that is still not a reason to fear them, or this. Whoever is sitting on you is feeding off your energy, and that can be dealt with. Contact someone who has experience in getting rid of such entities. Always trust your instincts because most of the time you are probably accurate. Not every time someone experiences catalepsy during sleep is there some dark entity feasting on an all-you-can-eat buffet, so just realize this before you get too worked up over it.

What is happening during this time is that the conscious mind has become aware of the soul and the sleeping body at the same time. At this moment you are conscious and if you wish, you can literally step out and leave on an astral journey and be in conscious control of it too. Freedom to go wherever you wish and see the world, or the stars, or whatever timeline suits your fancy. It is quite fun and liberating. In fact, many people do this once they realize this is possible, but please don't let fear take you over. This is your opportunity for astral freedom. This is freedom from the restrictions of this body and this dimension, and to experience the ability to come and go as you please. How very exciting! Instead of fear, this catalepsy is replaced with joy and control of yourself, your whole self, and the selves you have forgotten about. So, if this happens to you and your experience is fear, then stop just a moment and remind yourself what is happening. You simply are aware of your soul, which doesn't sleep, remind yourself of this, let go of fear, know you are safe and able to get up and leave. Try it! You can do this! You are not limited! Now go out there and fly!

Release Dreams: These are dreams that I must say are completely misunderstood. I say this because, according to dream research, these would be so-called random dreams such as crazy ones that seem to jump around and be disconnected and make zero sense. Like, first you were driving a car, then pigs were flying, and next you are in a castle and don't know how you got there. You know the crazy ones I speak of. It is widely believed that these dreams have no meaning whatsoever, and lending credibility to them is pretty much a waste of time. Scientifically speaking, it is also understood that our brain works like a computer, constantly taking in information, and when the memory is full it's time to clean out the files and make room for more information. Now I'm not a professional dream researcher, however, let's analyze this for a minute. Science has proven that the heart has just as many neurotransmitters as the brain, and in recent studies it's been proven that the heart and brain communicate in an equal two-way conversation, not only that, but it's done in four different ways; through the transmission of nerve cells, pressure waves, electromagnetically, and through hormones. Moreover, this communication significantly affects the brains activity. Yoga has been teaching this for thousands of years, if only the scientists who discovered this took more authentic yoga it would not have been such a recent breakthrough. But could this new science lend credibility to the idea that dreams are somehow connected with the heart equally as much as the brain? I guess at this point no one really knows for certain, but logic dictates it to not only be a possibility, and a credible one at that, but a high probability one as well. Does it not lend credibility that the heart and mind are taking part in our dreams in equal conjunction? Leaving it to the question, "Is this just a brain data dump?" I assure you, that nothing in all of creation is random and all dreams have a category that can be interpreted with, the exception of these dreams. So why would there be a group called release dreams that are considered just random data dumps from the brain that have no meaning? Just because it is not understood doesn't mean that it is some random junk, just like our DNA that had been dubbed as junk DNA due to lack of understanding. Now they are saying perhaps there is a significance to this unknown junk DNA. Together they still have much to be discovered and understood, but to label it as random junk until this understanding is discovered, I believe, is a grave mistake. I decided to ask my guides their take on this category of dreams, and this is what they had to say about it, as usual the answer is both interesting and curious.

They said that release is the wrong word to use for these dreams, and a more appropriate name for them would be transference dreams. Wow. Those two names aren't even close to each other. While one means let go of, the other means the action of transferring something, to move from one location to another. Hmm, now there's something to think about. During a transference dream we are transferring information from this self to the higher realms into your infinite storage device on an organic multi-phasic crystalline memory matrix. And, not only that, we are exchanging information with it during this type of dreaming, meaning information is flowing in both directions. Before you say our higher self, knows pretty much everything, where do you think your higher self, got some of this information about everything? We contribute knowledge to this memory matrix in every lifetime so, yes, we are all contributing to this through every incarnation. Even when your dog dreams he's contributing to this memory matrix. Moreover, we dream in layers, similar, to going up and down on an elevator and each floor being a dream within a dream just like the movie *"Inception,"* with *Leonardo DiCaprio*. Where do you think they got the idea for the movie? And we are aware of all the dreams at once, therefore, we seem to be jumping around in our dream and they have no relevance or connection to each other because we are trying to make a single experience out of many when we wake up and attempt to sort out and understand what seemingly weird stuff we do remember.

Prophetic Dreams: This dream category simply means that you dream of something before it happens. Example: My sister had a dream her friend was pregnant, and, as it turned out, her friend got pregnant the same night my sister had the dream. These dreams are not so cut and dried as my sisters dream was though. Example: In another dream my sister had was that she took her son, Kyle, to his dirt bike race the following morning and he wrecked his bike, resulting in a broken arm. The following day Kyle did have a dirt bike race, and as any mom would, she decided not to let him go to the race or ride his dirt bike that day to avoid the broken arm.

As it turned out, her other son, Ethan, was riding Kyle's dirt bike out back that day, wrecked it and broke his arm. While she did get a heads up on this, she was unable to prevent it because, you see, some experiences are just meant to happen. They are written in for a reason and not meant to be interfered with and this is a prime example of that. Know that prophetic dreams can come to anyone. While I have two sisters who are prophetic dreamers, and yes, they are psychic but, it is not necessarily only for psychic people. I am psychic and, as of this writing, have yet to have a prophetic dream ever in my lifetime. Some people may have them regularly, while others only on occasion, or perhaps only a one-time experience. There seems to be no rhyme or reason to it, other than what we do know is that everything has a rhyme and a reason. I must conclude, each, and every one of these prophetic dreams either were written into our life script or perhaps our guides decided it was necessary to give us this information for a reason. But, rest assured, even if the situation is something that must be experienced, you did not have this prophetic dream for no reason.

Daydreams: According to Wikipedia, daydreaming is a short-term detachment from one's immediate surroundings, during which a person's contact with reality is blurred and partially substituted by visions of fantasy. While this may be true, it lends to reason that one may ask as to why would we temporarily detach from our current reality during our waking hours? I decided this would be a good question to ask the guides, and this is what they have to say about it, which I am finding to be very interesting. "Day-dreaming almost always is caused by your guides literally tapping us out of this reality." Why would they do this? Daydreaming is similar, to astral traveling and caused by boredom, just as it is so often believed. The conscious mind loosens, you could say, from reality and, simply put, withdraws from the chains that bind you to this mind and body.

The so-called chains that hold the consciousness to this mind and body loosen so you can move up and out, and this, is why people may have a spiritual experience or see visions of things during this time. This also can be achieved through certain meditations. This is advised by the guides to do so in order to free your consciousness from these heavy chains that bind us to this current reality and assist us in connecting to our spiritual selves much easier. The reason children daydream more often than adults do is because they are closer to source than we are. This technique is used by the guides to tap both adults and children, but more commonly the children into the daydream in order to communicate with and help the daydreamer get their bearings in this space/time reality. We all come from a place where linear time doesn't exist, and we are still working on living in a reality created with time for our benefit in this experience. This is especially so for the children who have not been here as long. In short, the daydream allows you to distinguish between your physical reality and your astral reality. The point is that this is used to differentiate and balance the two. This is learned at a young age, like talking or reading, and tends to happen without thought as we get older. Therefore, daydreaming is necessary to grab a foothold, so to speak, on this reality and be capable of balance for the duration of time you are in this lifetime. So, now with this information, understand it is probably not a good idea to get after kids for daydreaming, or even adults for that matter. I used to daydream so much I hardly remember anything from third grade, except I was always daydreaming as I stared endlessly out the window of my classroom and my teacher was constantly complaining about it. Well, I turned out alright in the end, so all my daydreaming didn't hurt me too bad. Definitely; not near as much as this reality did.

Nightmares: Let's face it, we have all had that horrifying nightmare, whether on occasion or as a regular occurrence, at least at some point in our lives. While nightmares can be terrifying, there is hope for resolving such situations on most occasions. These dreams are often a collection of many things manifesting into your dream world and they are often like other dreams where there is an unresolved issue that needs to be addressed, either from a past life or this life. Example: I have a sister that has been plagued throughout her life by a dream about dying in a red car, when, she did die in a red car in a past life, or as we understand death anyway. Once the conscious mind realizes this was another lifetime, and not this one, a dream such as this can be resolved and no longer resonates with the consciousness of the dreamer. At this point, these dreams tend to cease their occurrence and give some level of peace in the dream state. Nightmares also can occur from a traumatic event, or events, we have experienced or currently are experiencing on a regular basis. This can either be because you have not moved forward from it, or because the dream is telling you to be aware of what's really happening in your life and it's time to do something about it. Once we understand many of these dreams, we realize they are simply telling us to deal with it and move forward from it rather than continued fear or anxiety, or any other negative emotion or pattern that goes along with it. Such a traumatic dream can be acknowledged and released, ultimately releasing the trauma causing it in the first place. Another reason for our nightmares is that we do often astral travel to lower dimensions in our sleep, and this can be a very disturbing experience. There, we experience things that perhaps might reflect what hell would be, if there was such a place. I have seen many artist's renditions of their dreams when visiting such places, The famous artist, *Zdzislaw Beksinski*, is one such artist whose artwork is a depiction of the lower dimensions. And it is also good to realize we ourselves are in a lower dimension. I mean the third dimension is pretty, low on the totem pole: with all of the negativity, violence, war, crime and abuse in this dimension, anyone astral traveling here from a higher dimension than ours would think they came into a chaos of hell, too. Imagine being from a higher dimension where love, giving and harmony are almost constant, with very little conflict or disagreement, and then you, astral travel to WWI or WWII in Auschwitz! How frightening would that be? Pretty horrifying, I would think.

Some dreams you might classify as nightmares are not such. Let's say you dream about blood, or a dead, grotesque body. While this may seem quite disturbing, it may very well be bringing you a message. Blood and death generally carry a message of a rebirth, or change coming rather than doom and gloom headed your way. This change could be a major one like a move to another state, or something minor like a move to the next office. There's no real way to predict what change is coming, but when you have such dreams replace fear with knowledge, and there is nothing to worry about. You see, even nightmares can be understood, and misplaced fear can be overcome in order to release the negative connotation with such dreams.

I am going to mention this nightmare, just because this can happen, it does not necessarily mean it is happening to you, so please, before I get into the negative entity thing, you absolutely have no reason for fear, and you absolutely do have control over your reality and your dream world. There are negative entities who can manipulate your dreams and create nightmares. I experienced one when I was fifteen and living in a house with a dark creepy entity that enjoyed creating nightmares within my dream time, as well as creating fear within the home and feeding off our energy frequency. Once I became an adult and an experienced psychic, I did go back to that house in an astral state and cleared it right out. He's no longer there. If this is what might be happening to you in your dreams, there are two things you can do. Number one, as already mentioned in this book, put up your protection barriers before going to sleep and say your affirmations. Number two, put black Obsidian pyramids under the bed to keep the creeper out from under there, because that is often their favorite place to hide while manipulating dreams. And number three, please call someone who has experience in getting rid of such things, and again, I don't mean they will sage and leave, but send this being back to source. You can sage yourself, and dark entity or not, please create the habit of smudging the house regularly. Yes, this is just beginner level stuff and I have many more tools in my toolbox for such situations, but one has to start somewhere, and this is a great place to do so.

Symbolic Dreams: This would be the dream I have the most often, and this is probably true for most people. The difference between the symbolic dreams and release dreams is that the symbolic dream seems to have an order to it, while the release dreams seem to jump around with no rhyme or reason. In these symbolic dreams there are messages, some are messages from your subconscious or higher self, or Angels, or even loved ones. All may be true for a symbolic dream and may come from any of them who are in constant contact with you. But, regardless of who is sending them, these dreams are very significant and should be written down immediately. By writing these dreams down you can decipher their meaning quite easily. I strongly suggest keeping a dream dictionary by your bed for this purpose. I personally have the *"Dream Dictionary" by Rose Inserra*, which I find to be quite good, however, there are many good dream dictionaries out there that will serve your purpose very well. Just trust that the right one for you will show up when you go looking for it. By writing the dream itself, and then breaking it up into individual symbols, and writing the meanings of each symbol down you will be able to easily analyze and decipher the symbolic meaning of your own dream. Not only will you be able to understand your own dream patterns better, but possibly learn to assist others in deciphering their dreams. If you are still perplexed and unable to find resolution to a dream that is really bothering you, for answers then I recommend contacting a psychic that is good at dream interpretation. Remember, just because they are psychic doesn't mean dreams are their thing, so I suggest asking specifically if they do dream interpretations before going to that person. That person may be great at something else, while dreams just might not be their strong suit.

Here is an example of a symbolic dream I had many years

ago. It was a clear and beautiful night with a full moon bright as can be. I was walking through a forest of pines in the mountains and everything was covered in snow. It was a deep snow that was difficult to walk through, and it created a great struggle for me to get through. It was a very vivid dream and when I woke up, even though I distinctly could feel the cold and the deepness of the snow, I felt quite comfortable and at home in this location. I was not at all concerned with hiking through the woods on a full moon, knee deep in snow and not a house or road anywhere in sight, freezing in the cold. No, I felt perfectly comfortable and at home in this situation. Let's break this dream down. The moon means an aspect of myself is coming to the surface, and a full moon means a wholeness or completeness within myself, which probably would explain the comfortable feeling of being in this situation. Second, we have a forest of pine trees. This represents my unconsciousness which is exactly where I was at the time, unable to see the big picture because I was only focused on the current situation. And lastly, the deep heavy snow that was difficult to walk through means things being covered up or hidden. This was true. I was hiding the fact that I am psychic from the world at this time. This dream was telling me that I was unconscious, unable to see the big picture, while hiding my true authentic self from the world and it was time for another aspect of me to emerge and eventually bring my whole self to the forefront from this place where I was. Which I did. Slowly, but I did. Some dreams may make sense right away, while others may take a while to fully comprehend, but either way, this is an important step for understanding not only your dreams but a true and authentic deeper you than you already are aware of even.

Recurring Dreams: These dreams are exactly what the name implies. These dreams come back over, and over again over a matter of days, weeks, months, or even years. There is no rule as to how long they tend to last, only that they seem to come back again and again. And, every kind of dream can be a recurring dream because it simply means to come back. I had a dream about a house that was in horrible disrepair, and each room was worse than the one before. I mean tearing it down and starting over would be a better financial decision than to repair it, yet as I walked through the house from room to room, I kept telling myself, "I can fix this," as well as in my mind see the room completely redone, updated and beautiful. As this dream continued over several years, the house seemed to require less and less work and some of the rooms were new looking while others were still untouched and falling apart. Then less and less work was required each time I had the dream. Eventually, my house was beautiful. This happened over a five-year time span. What did this recurring dream mean? I now know the house represents me, and the destroyed rooms represent what was going on inside of me. And, little by little, as I repaired and understood myself, I also began to little by little, repair and understand my house. Once I was where I needed to be, the dreams stopped. So too with your recurring dreams, be they from a past, life memory, symbolic, or whatever, once you no longer need the understanding of the dreams, then they too, will discontinue.

Now that we have learned how to categorize, log, and, with assistance of the dream dictionary, interpret our dreams, I do believe it's possible to clarify and understand most of your dreams. I do believe it is safe to say that there's no such thing as just a dream. In fact, our dreams are a very significant part of our spirit selves, and by better understanding them we have a better understanding of our self as well.

CHAPTER EIGHT

UNDERSTANDING THE BASIC USE OF CRYSTALS

People often think of psychics and believe that we have a crystal ball to gaze into and see the future. If only that were true! While we often do work with crystals, and it is true that a crystal in a sphere shape is very powerful, unfortunately, simply looking into a large crystal and seeing your future is a complete fabrication unless there is somebody out there who knows something I don't. Or, perhaps, some super advanced technology with crystals might achieve this sometime in the distant future of humanity. But for now, we will stick to what we do know about crystals.

While there are some misguided conceptions regarding crystals and the use of them, there's still plenty of true and accurate information available. As it appears, our ancestors were well aware of the power crystals wield. They have been using crystals for thousands of years, if not longer, which most likely is the case. Yes, crystals have been used by our ancestors for everything from curing diseases to assisting on the battlefield.

In the Bible, it is mentioned in the book of *Genesis*, for example, that crystals were used in temples and on breastplates for the priests. Yet the use of crystals dates back much farther than the Bible. It seems humans have had an infinity for crystals since our creation. Talismans and amulets with crystals have been found in many archeological dig sites dating back thousands of years from Europe, to Asia, to South America, and everywhere in between. In fact, the oldest known amulets, thus far, were made of amber and date back

30,000 years. Discoveries in Britain, date crystal use from 10,000 years ago. In the Si'nai' peninsula there are malachite mines dating back to 4,000 B.C., and crystals have also been found in Paleolithic gravesites in parts of Switzerland and Belgium.

Ancient Sumerians have historical records of using them. It seems everything modern, when researched, the Ancient Sumerians seemed to have knowledge of almost everything from astrology to math to DNA, so why not crystals? Most likely they were the ones to introduce crystals and their uses to the ancient Egyptians, who used stones like lapis lazuli, turquoise, carnelian, emeralds, and clear quartz as a part of their daily life, and they were often placed in jewelry.

The ancient Greeks accredited many attributes to crystal use, and even most modern names we have today for our crystals can be traced back to origins from the Greek language.

It's no secret that Jade was highly valued in ancient Chinese culture, while in South America masks made of Jade were discovered dating around 250 years ago, lending credit to the idea that South American cultures had value in it as well. Even the Maori people of New Zealand wore Jade pendants to show respect for their ancestor's spirits. While the Zuni of North America would carve turquoise animals to represent animal totems, or animal spirits, most Native American tribes hold crystals as sacred, especially turquoise.

It is interesting how crystals seem to have the same, or very similar, uses by so many ancient cultures around the world who presumably had no contact with each other. Jaspers, for example seem to almost always be used for its calming effects as well as assisting the user in finding strength.

It seems not only our ancient ancestors of the common population used crystals, but the clergy as well, because they have been represented in all major religions around the world. Crystals are mentioned in the Bible, Tora, and Koran, and in the Hindu religion. The Hindu's much-venerated Kalpa Tree is said to be made completely of precious gems, while a Buddhist text from the 7th century mentions a diamond throne, as well as a long list of many other religious texts mentioning the use of crystals. The Roman Catholic church put a ban on all crystal talismans and amulets in 355 A.D., yet the bishops and other ecclesiastic figures continued to wear them in the form of other jewelry, including rings.

Using crystals as a healing tool can easily be found in antiquity from the Dark Ages all the way through the Renaissance era. People often used crystals in every type of healing in conjuncture with herbal remedies. That is, it seems, until the late 1600's when a man named *Thomas Nicole* expressed in his *"Faithful Lapidary"* that gems were only inanimate objects, therefore could not possibly possess the abilities claimed in the past. This seems to be the beginning of the end for the use of crystals and other precious stones in healing and protection, as well as anything else one might use the crystals for. However, during the early 1900's a number of interesting experiments were conducted on a variety of different people to study the effects crystals may have on a person. The results seem to have produced similar experiences between many of the test subjects. Still this seems to be not enough to send the general public reeling back to the common use of them in the way our ancestors did. During the 1980's crystals seem to have begun re-emerging in popularity while being used for many things, including both physical and emotional healing.

I have seen and experienced this energy first-hand. Crystal therapy may be making a slow comeback, as far as mainstream goes, however, they are making a comeback with more and more people using them. This idea is slowly but surely becoming more widely accepted, as an alternative method of healing.

How does this crystal energy healing really work anyway? Well, Quartz, for example, has the unique ability to convert electrical energy into mechanical energy. This is called the piezo-electric effect and it means to transform one type of energy into another. For example, in the case of the quartz crystal it turns electrical energy into mechanical energy, which can be focused and directed.

Because of the powerful energy crystals have, they are essential to our modern technology. They are in everything we use from watches and clocks to cell phones, radios, computers, even LED stands for liquid crystal display. Silicon even is made from using crystals. Galena and pyrite can be used to make radio receivers that do not require the use of batteries, while rubies were used in the first laser developed by Bell Laboratories in the 1960's and are still used in lasers today.

Crystals have been proven to oscillate (vibrate) at their own frequencies and even respond to the input of vibrations. A device called the crystal central oscillator is used to change frequency of radio waves. Rochelle salt crystal works in this manner to the highest degree while quartz has the greatest mechanical strengths, although Tourmaline has also been proven to work for this purpose also. Due to the uniqueness of how crystals are structured, they respond to the input of many different energies around them causing them to oscillate and emit specific vibratory frequencies. So too do the cells of the human body oscillate at certain frequencies, as do our chakras and dantians (energy vortexes of the human body) creating a cause and effect of crystal and human cell vibrations interacting. As they begin to vibrate together, so too will the healing of the human crystalline structure take place.

According to *"Book of Stones," by Robert Simmons*, which is considered one of the most in-depth books on crystals ever written, *"When we bring the crystal into our electromagnetic field, two things occur: The electromagnetic frequencies carried by the stones will vibrate with related frequencies in our own energy field. The nervous system is attuned to these shifts in energy and transmits this information to the brain. Here the frequencies stimulate biochemical shifts that effect the physical body and shift brain function." (Simmons & Ahsian 2005, 28)*

We see how and why crystals have the ability, to work with the human body for healing purposes, but how is it that they are able, to assist us in our spiritual growth? That is simple. Energy, frequency and vibration is the answer. Remember that *Nikola Tesla* said these are the keys to understanding the universe.

Crystals are millions of years old forged during the earliest time in Earth's (aka; Gaia) development. This delicate stage gave us a bounty of magical and amazing crystals to work with us, not necessarily for us but with us in a partnership. These crystals have a powerful ability to help us heal both physically and emotionally, as well as retain memories and data. They hold, retrieve and store information that work within your own energy frequency. The truth is that you also must be doing the work to heal. If you have anxiety and are working hard to overcome it, then a crystal such as amethyst will assist in calming your anxiety. They work like a partner with you and they too have the ability to feel love. In fact, the more love energy that is projected into them, the more powerful they become in their abilities to assist you.

The consciousness of the crystals can be transferrable from human consciousness to the crystal, and vice versa. I personally did not know exactly how this works but through my automatic writing I was told this information. When I asked if it works like Superman's crystals in the movie, they said, "yes, exactly like Superman's crystals." I since then have successfully downloaded my consciousness into a clear quartz crystal. It was done with Angelic assistance, and I don't think I could repeat it again at the time of this writing without their help.

And, not only that, but each crystal knows whose energy it can work with and whose it can't. Therefore the crystals "call" you, as I refer to it. It is quite common to walk into a crystal shop for one type of crystal, feel attracted to another and get that one. That crystal was calling you. They are singing your song, your song of creation to get your attention. According to my automatic writing from my guides, this is how intelligent and advanced they are. There is much more to the crystals than we humans know, however, we are not advanced enough yet in our understanding to truly use them to their fullest potential. We may be only babies, as far as our spiritual growth goes, and are only just learning to crawl with these stones, not yet ready to walk, let alone run, but that is okay. Let's crawl for now and learn what we are ready for. This will lead us, and future generations into the greater understanding of what we are capable of doing with such magnificent sentient beings such as these beautiful crystals.

There are so many crystals that volumes of crystal encyclopedias, dictionaries and books have been written. There are so many good ones to choose from that I am hardly doing crystals justice by giving them only one chapter.

Due to the vastness of how many crystals are out there, and their amazing qualities, I will limit my list below to just a few of the most common ones that are easy to find to start working with. These are some of the must-have crystals to start out with, as well as, for every advanced crystal worker out there.

Black Tourmaline: This is one of my favorites to work with and I absolutely had to include it. This is a good crystal for empaths to use, and if you are an empath, get one and you will know why I say this. This is a strong protection stone and often carried to keep negative energies and entities at bay. Black tourmaline is also a powerful grounding stone due to the fact, that it is electrical in nature. It creates a strong connection between human and Earth (Gaia). This might be why it also assists in calming panic attacks. It is often used to balance energies within the body, while providing a healing light through the energy channels of the human body. This crystal is quite popular due to its versatile nature and while most commonly it comes in the shade of black it often can come in blue- even blue so dark that it may appear black. I must say the green and pink varieties are quite attractive, and while more difficult to find, they are out there and have some varied qualities from the black or dark blue variety. This crystal works well with the Root Chakra and meditation on the Earth mother.

Obsidian: This is a strong protective stone that shields against negative energy and entities which is why I recommend keeping black obsidian pyramids under the bed. It also blocks psychic attack and absorbs negative energy from the environment. This stone also works well with the first chakra known as the Root Chakra. Apache Tears also known as snowflake obsidian are another form of obsidian that has grey, or white splashes on them. These work the same as regular obsidian.

Blood Stone: This stone is a dark green with drops of red in it that may remind you of blood drops, hence the name. This is a good healing stone for people with blood issues. It heightens intuition and enhances creativity. It draws off negative energy and is good for assisting people in reducing stress. This stone may be used with either the first chakra (Root) or the second chakra (Sacral) This is a good stone for people who are very artistic in nature.

Orange and Red Carnelian: These beautiful and vibrant stones are commonly used to assist in finding courage, and strength, while building energy levels and endurance, which is why it's often carried by athletes. Plus, they often aid architects and builders because it is said to assist in ideas, motivation, drive and determination, which may be why it is considered a stone that also attracts prosperity. This stone works well with the second chakra known as the Sacral Chakra.

Orange and Coral Calcite: Commonly used with the Root (first chakra) sacral (second chakra) Solar Plexus (third chakra) and Heart (fourth chakra). These stones help to draw in a high vibration of divine love while transmuting negative emotions to more powerful loving and joyous emotions. An excellent choice for those who have past traumas to heal from. It assists the self in pushing forward for the healing process.

Tigers Eye: This beauty really does look like a glass tiger's eye with its amber brown color and beautifully striped essence that looks varied in depth. It is often used to assist in strength, stealth, balance, vitality, and willpower. They assist with focusing and creating mental clarity, as well as helping to resolve issues objectively with limited emotional interference. This stone may be used for protection and commonly works with the Root (first chakra) and Solar Plexus (third chakra). This is a good one to use in dispelling fear and anxiety.

Citrine: What a beauty this one is coming in a variety of yellow, orange, or brownish colors, which is created by heating. Yellow is the most natural and common you will find. They are in the quartz family and probably can be categorized as one of the most popular crystals. Citrine is a spiritual cleansing stone and is often used as a balancing stone when your energies are "off". They are excellent for assisting in self-improvement and self-healing, as well as increasing energy and drive to pick up the pieces and start again if you have experienced loss, grief, trauma, or a recent unexpected life change. Citrine carries the power of the sun, therefore, if you wish to feel sunny and cheerful again citrine is the one for you. Citrine works with the solar plexus (third chakra) and is an excellent crystal to help you with fears, phobias and depression because they often can make you look forward to the future with hope and optimism. They help you go with the flow, so to speak, while drawing out the doom and gloom.

Rose Quartz: This wonderful and beautiful pink quartz crystal works well with the Heart Chakra (fourth chakra). This crystal is the most common for healing heart pain while promoting self-love, friendship and deep inner, feelings of peace and harmony. This crystal carries feminine energy of compassion, and also can be used to ward off bad dreams while promoting a peaceful sleep and may assist with fears of the dark. It also promotes proper functioning of the heart, tensions and stress.

Green Aventurine: While aventurine does come in a multitude of colors, I am only including the green variety in order to avoid this from getting too ridiculously long. This stone is used with the Heart Chakra (fourth chakra). It is used to resolve blockages and to rebalance the Heart Chakra. It often helps us to understand our own needs and find balance within those needs. It is a good one to assist with change and flow; but is also known as the lucky stone and is commonly known to bring in abundance by placing the bearer in positions that bring about good opportunities. This is an all-around healing stone that may assist with the lungs, heart, liver, sinuses and to loosen and release negative energy.

Lapis Lazuli: A very beautiful blue stone with the power to open your Throat Chakra (fifth chakra). This is an excellent stone for executives, journalists, inventors, writers and teachers. But overall, this is the must-have stone for Angel communicators (this is what psychics are called on the Other Side). This stone assists with communication and the speaking of your own truth. The truth and honesty of the spirit comes out when using this one. It assists with smooth and even communication, especially for those who tend to argue or feel misunderstood. It attracts positivity, success and promotion.

Sodalite: Another blue beauty, and while this one works very similar as the lapis lazuli, it also works with the Throat Chakra and Third Eye (sixth chakra). This crystal assists with enhancing intuition by working with the pituitary gland, which is your connection to your intuition and psychic self. It also helps us to be calm when weathering the storms of life. It is a good crystal to use for stress and tiredness. They often help with the adrenal gland, the gland associated with your psychic or intuition abilities.

Amethyst: This pretty-purple quartz is commonly used with both the Third Eye (sixth chakra) and the Crown Chakra (seventh chakra). Common healing uses would be the nervous system as well as nightmares and insomnia, depression, and anxiety. Amethyst is used to calm, protect and cleanse the spirit. It strengthens intuition, psychic abilities and meditation.

Clear Quartz: This is the most powerful healing stone there is. It is the generic crystal of the crystal world and can be used for anything listed above and then some. I always suggest to people just getting into crystals to get some clear quartz, because when in doubt of what crystal to use, then this one will work. It assists in tuning into your higher self and assists in relieving pain. It is sometimes called the master healer and will amplify energy and thought, as well as the effect of other crystals. Yes, anytime you pair it with another crystal, or crystals, then the quartz will enhance the abilities of whatever crystal you pair it with. This stone can be used with any of the seven chakras.

Selenite: Here is another wonderful crystal that everyone should get when starting out with crystals. Aside from its beauty, this crystal is commonly known for many mystical and healing properties. They assist in mental clarity and quiets a very active mind. They protect you from psychic attack and can balance and stabilize bodily energy, as well as emotions. This stone is the one to use to assist you on your spiritual enlightenment journey. It can be used to awaken, or strengthen, your telepathic abilities. They can also be used for connecting with Angels and spirit guides. Additionally, they may be used for healing the skeletal system like arthritis, cancer, tumors, and the clearing of glands. They remove blockages in your field and cleanses your aura of all toxins that affect the physical body. Selenite is an excellent partner for meditations.

It is important to know that you be aware of how to take care of your new crystals. As soon as you get new crystals and even every so often you should clear your crystals, which means to clean all of the energy off of them. This can be done in many ways. The most common way is to use sage, but they can be cleared with selenite. Or by putting them in a bowl of rice overnight. If you choose to do this, then please throw the rice away. Water from Gaia (Earth) can also clear your crystals, either creek water, waterfalls, or even the ocean, but some crystals can't be put in water, such as calcite or angelite. Know that tap water does not cleanse crystals, however, I do use crystals to cleanse tap water. I personally keep a water pitcher in the refrigerator with crystals in it for drinking. And it tastes amazing. Be careful because not all crystals work together, so make sure the ones you put into the pitcher are a good match. Your crystals will require to be charged on occasion as well. The best way to charge crystals is either put them under the full moon, or sunlight for at least a few hours. Also, selenite can charge other crystals. Taking good care of your crystals is important. And by all means; please project love into them. They absolutely can feel it and it does enhance their ability.

Now that you are ready to move forward and purchase some crystals, where do you get these wonderful crystals? It often depends on where you live. For example, here in Arizona, there are many crystal shops, as well as world renowned crystal shows like Tucson and Quartzite where people and crystals come from all over the world. If you do not have many crystal shops nearby, perhaps you do have a crystal show like the one in Denver Colorado every September, which is one of the biggest in the country. If there are no crystal shows near you then, perhaps, there is an opportunity to go dig your own crystals, like Wegner Quartz crystal mines in Arkansas. If this is not an option, then there is the Internet, however, I will caution that some crystals are not authentic, especially ones coming from China. While there are authentic crystals that do come from China, often they are just painted glass and one must be cautious. I recommend looking for an authentic crystal shop here in the United States with an authentic website, a real retail shop, and phone number. Absolutely cleanse these crystals immediately upon receiving them. Go ahead and get yourself some crystals and begin to understand the power and love they have to share with you.

As we move forward into a new golden age of humanity, we are absolutely going to see the emergence of more and more crystal healing centers and more healers practicing the art of crystal healing. We will see more people incorporating them into their daily lives as they learn to not just understand the benefits of working with the crystals, but they will begin to feel the crystals in ways they never thought possible. An entirely new experience and understanding of the self, universe, energy, and power is created once crystals become introduced into your life. You will never be the same again.

CHAPTER NINE

UNDERSTANDING MY OWN ABILITIES

I must say it has been quite a road to get this far, and for all my research and experiences accumulated over the years, I honestly did not expect things to bring me to where I am now. I have received much help from my Angels and Guides in writing this book, and they have told me this chapter should focus on my own abilities, which I must say was not my intention, but here goes. I am an empath with clairaudience, clairsentience, claircognitive, clairvoyance, clairgustance, clairolfaction, clairtangency, and clairempathy abilities. So that means I am a clear hearing, seeing, feeling and knowing Empath who occasionally smells or tastes something but not my strongest abilities which I am okay with. I do travel through dimensions and can experience clairtangency. I also do automatic writing and I am a direct voice channeler which means I actually step out of my body and allow a channel to speak through me using their own voice. I also have experienced psychometry. I hear some words when healing horses and dogs while using my other abilities to offer a reading on them as well. I am an energy healer for people, dogs, horses and property. If being a healer interests you, I do offer healing schools. We are all energy and we all have the ability, to be a healer and we are all psychic we must use and further develop these abilities.

Those of us the world calls psychic, have a high vibratory gene that makes it easier to access, however, there is not a human alive that doesn't have the ability to train their own abilities, it just requires working hard. Believe me, it is there. And this information came directly from my guides, so I personally trust it completely.

What might you experience from an energy healing with me? Well, I am constantly learning and advancing my skills, so most likely, it will continue to change and continue to advance. Future healings may be quite different than my current offerings. But my current healings generally will be like this, first I cleanse your auric field with Kyanite, and sound. This is something I teach everyone to do, and strongly advise it to be done regularly. I use crystal pyramids to create a beautiful sound healing over the body, to search for energy blockages and to run a healing sound frequency through the body. I begin my routine of clearing and balancing your dantians, the three major energy channels that T'ai-Chi teaches us. Then, I will open and align 13 of your chakras. Then I clear your central energy channel which is an energy tube that runs down the center of your head through the center of your body and through your perineum (the soft spot in front of the anus) into the earth. If you put your forefinger and thumb together that should be about the size of your central channel. After I clear blockages from your central channel, I then will clear your meridian lines. If you have ever seen that poster in an acupuncture office of the human body with all of the energy lines running through it and showing the positions indicating where to stick the needles in, those are your meridian lines. I also will do a cranium alignment and run energy down your spine, then wrap it around your hips. If I get a knowing to work extra on a location, or if the client mentions a specific location that has given them problems, I will give it extra attention by running extra energy through that location. I use colors for healing by projecting in my mind's eye the appropriate color to the appropriate location as I am working on someone. I also use sound healing, meaning I hum or sing the song of the colors I am using. My guides taught me how to do this. Whatever I remove energetically I also replace with positive love energy. I work on a cellular and DNA level which means sometimes it pulls up like a screen in front of me, it looks like the computer screen Iron Man uses. Also, there are times a full mediumship reading will come through while I am working or some visions of a past life that requires healing something that is affecting your current life. I offer this healing at my healing center Halo's Holistic Healing Center in Mesa; Arizona I also am available to do this work remotely. I seal the energy into your energy field when I am finished. My program is very similar with the dogs and horses as well.

I also do land clearing and healing. Land can receive trauma too and requires energy healing just like humans and animals, I offer the land clearing from my own location unless I feel very strongly that I must go to the property in person.

When I am working with the land, I will first scan it and locate who, or what is causing the disturbances. I can do this remotely. I must know where I am going so pictures and location help. Once I know where I am headed, I then go into a meditative state where I connect to the property. I can see the entire premises on an energetic level and find whomever is residing there be they positive or negative, and this includes the energy of the place as well. I then proceed to send them up to the Angel realm or help them cross over or send them back to the dimension they came from or whatever my guides tell me is the best move for the being I am dealing with, be they positive or negative. The Angels will give them the proper healing they deserve or decide if they are unable to be healed and should be returned to source where they belong. At this point they cease to exist as a separate entity and once again become an energy of pure light. I will then cleanse the house, with a pure white light of love, and set a permanent intention of love, joy, inspiration, gratitude, wonder and prosperity to all who live on the premises. Then I will put up a barrier of energy to seal in the work that I did to repel anything dark from entering the property again. I also teach my clients how to properly cleanse and put up their own barriers, empowering them to feel strong and safe and to refuse to be a victim of negative entities or energy.

If the property is discovered to have a gateway or portal, I must say that in most cases if you are dealing with this situation, I must recommend that you just move. Also, I would like to say that not all gateways, are meant to be shut down nor are they all bad.

On the Other Side, we are not called psychics but Angel communicators which I like better. My friend Maryann calls my readings life readings because I am helping you with the current life path you are on and help you to take control of your future life path yourself. I often talk to the Angels, guides, loved ones who crossed over and even pets. Also, the term psychic has derived such a negative connotation over the centuries and even to this day, we still hear all sorts of misguided understandings of what we do. Many miss the fact that each of us may experience things quite differently from each other, while having similar or the same abilities. A certain idea of what we are capable has arisen from content in books and from Hollywood that are quite unrealistic. I would like to clarify what I do during a reading. Or, perhaps, I should say what I don't do. I am not a fortune teller. I do not give you a reading on your future, and here is why. Many years ago I asked the guides why they refuse to answer any of my questions regarding the future, and their answer was that we have many branches written into our script that we wrote ourselves and if they tell us one branch, we will tend to go down that branch instead of realizing we have choices and can actually choose for ourselves which one to take. This is against the law of free will, therefore, they do not talk about the future on a personal level. They have answered questions on a more general planetary level, although they rarely will answer in a manner of time. Usually, they will tell me "soon," 99% of the time. I will answer your question right now as to when something will happen that you are concerned about. Soon, or when it is supposed to. So, there is your professional psychic answer to your question. What I do during a reading is more like psychic therapy. I use all my abilities to assist in helping clients get on, and stay on, their spiritual path. I strongly encourage questions because the answers come directly from guides or Angels who will tell you that, due to free will, you must ask the question in order to get the answer. If you think because I am psychic, you should not have to ask me any questions you are wrong about how this works. The guides will only answer what you ask and nothing more. Believe me, we have been doing Q&A sessions with them for years and I cannot get them to answer anything I don't ask directly. Sometimes though I get lucky and ask the right question, which will lead to a 20-minute rant on educating humanity in the ways of doing things.

Another thing is that I do not control who, or what, comes through. Once I had two sisters come because they missed their loved grandpa who passed away, yet for almost thirty minutes there were Angels who came to bring messages to only one of the sisters while the other one was getting unhappy about the reading. Grandpa finally showed up and stated that there was no way he could get through because the Angels wanted to talk, and they were going to have their say before him, or anyone else. It did turn into a positive reading by the end of things, however, I have no idea if something like this example will happen. Yes, quite often, loved ones who have passed do come forward, but there have been times that they have not, which is why I do not promise this will happen, even though it often does.

One time I did a group reading for a family who lost their father. While information came out on some of the members along with a long list of other family members, who have passed away that decided to show-up to include a distant cousin they were not even close to, then just when I was about to finish up (and even I thought Dad was not going to show up) he did make an appearance at the very end. There is just no guarantee who will appear, and who will not, and there is no way of telling what kind of information I will get. If it is not what you want to hear, it doesn't mean you are not supposed to hear it. One thing I have learned is that they never waste your time, or my time, by giving us information that is not supposed to be given. If your Angels, or guides, tell me something for you, it is because they feel it is important for you to know. Therefore, I encourage people to take notes, or even record their reading, so they can remember these things. Once I did an energy healing and a reading on two horses when their owner, a very nice girl, mentioned her grandma had passed away. Then I hear "Rose." I asked her what that meant, and she said she had no idea, so I presumed perhaps Grandma wanted to give her a rose or had roses or something like this. Then the girl mentions Aunt Rose, whom I immediately connected to and was able to relay some very disturbing information in regards, to Aunt Rose. The girl did confirm most of it was accurate, yet some of it was very new knowledge to her, and yet, not surprising given the history of this woman who had zero regard for anyone, other than herself, and was very cruel to Grandma her last years of life. See, the word rose ended up being a person, who was not even a rose. Sometimes when something comes through it may take us days or weeks, or even months, for it to be understood and therefore I strongly encourage note taking. Think life coaching and intuitive therapist, with information from the Other Side, when you come see me. I honestly am here to help people get on their true spiritual life path and find happiness by creating their own wonderful, loving future full of abundance and spiritual understanding. People often book private sessions with me to help them better develop their own psychic abilities as well. Which I am happy to do.

Most people who seek out a psychic will do so because they are struggling in their lives and do not know where to turn, they are hoping we will give them a future of better things to come. I not only give messages from the Other Side to help get you on the right track, but I help with giving you tools to fight off depression, and advise on how to create that future you are looking for, rather than whether or not I can see a future full of happiness. I promise, it is far more useful to let me teach you how to take control of your own future and fill it with happiness with help and guidance from your Angels, guides, and loved ones. They have a greater understanding than you or I do as to your life path and soul journey. If it is within your life purpose, you can manifest it and bring it into your reality.

I do promise you that being depressed and miserable is not your life path, nor is continuing to beat yourself up over mistakes, or allow others to do it for you. It is impossible to grow and thrive under such circumstances.

I teach this with my master manifesting class, where I also talk about blockages and how to remove them. Once you get your energies right, and flush out the negativity, you change your energy field and only then are you capable of attracting better people, a better career and more money, as well as a more loving life partner, into your life.

Life coaching would include taking my master manifesting class to learn how to control your own energy field, energy healing, life readings, a past/other life regression as well as learning how to remove blockages through meditations. It's the entire package that will help you get your life on track, ditch the old negative patterns out the door and welcome in the possibility for new and exciting things to come.

What happens during a life regression? Many surprises and new things happen almost every time so, as soon as I say how it will go down, then something new happens, however, I can give a general description. First, I will talk you into a meditative state where you will be fully aware of what is going on and what you are experiencing. Usually, I will take you through three lifetimes where you tell me what you are remembering as you travel through these lives. Often, we may find issues that should be addressed since sometimes these issues will crossover into the current lifetime. By addressing and releasing these issues it can be very liberating to let go of fears, phobias, and what seems to be unfounded concerns and worries or even chronic physical pain. Example: If you are absolutely terrified of dogs, yet never have had a bad experience with them, it may very well be you were attacked by a dog, or wolf in a different lifetime. Or, perhaps no matter what you do you just cannot seem to manage your money, even though you have taken money management classes and always put something in savings.

You may have a good paying career, or work two jobs, yet you just cannot seem to get the money in order. Then you discover you were rich in a past life from ill-gotten gains and karma has decided to come for a call. This doesn't mean you have to stay in a financial bind to pay back your Karmic debt to the universe, but now that you know what it is, it can be addressed as an energy block that can be acknowledged and fixed. This doesn't mean if you have money problems that this is the reason, because the reasons are endless, and each person has their own individual reasons to address. Once these blockages from other lifetimes are located, they can be released bringing healing and joy into the current lifetime you are now in. After we go through lives, I often will take you to a nice meadow or beach where perhaps your guides or loved ones that have passed show up. I have even seen animal totems, pets, and Angels arrive. Again, I am not able to promise who will arrive, or what message they might bring, but I can promise that whatever it is it will be significant for you individually. Even if it's just a symbol, or sometimes just an acknowledgement of who they are, so you can begin to work with them yourself. These are all significant and profound connections that should be acknowledged and appreciated.

Now what are energy blocks? Besides the stress, worry and trauma that causes the energy blockages I clear out during an energy healing, we have many other types of blockages that have been created from other lifetimes, this lifetime, or even your ancestors blocks that you inherited. Yes, you can inherit their traumas just like their eye or hair color. Example: your dad was abusive, and you then dated an abusive guy, only to finally leave him and marry an abusive guy. This seems like a well-worn pattern I know, but what is causing this pattern? Perhaps it is learned from this life, perhaps from many lives, or perhaps many generations of women have done this, and it was inherited. No worries though because regardless of where it came from it absolutely is fixable. Physics proves this cycle will continue to repeat itself unless you change it. Remember, nothing will change until you change it and an energy pattern of this magnitude requires something equal to, or greater than, the energy that created it. What exactly does this mean? You are responsible for acknowledging and changing this cycle of energy is what this means, and when you change it then your entire life begins to change. Here's the catch, most likely there are many layers to these energy blockages and getting through them all is quite the challenge, but the change is something you should begin to see and feel as each one of these blockages are released.

As these layers are uncovered, bit by bit, a new and improved you will begin to emerge. One that is more advanced and understands the self, and higher self, on a more advanced and spiritual nature. Once on this path, there is no turning back from it. You will continue to advance yourself and find a path of life that you never thought was possible, and as you continue to advance you will be surprised at how there's no stopping it. Nor do you really want to because your life continues to improve and change on a regular basis as this goes on.

As you continue to advance spiritually with a spiritual life coach, you will begin to see miraculous things happen. One of those things will be the negative people in your life will seem to separate from you, as well as new positive and loving non-judgmental friends begin to appear. You also will begin to see an abundance of everything begin to appear, more and more, in your daily life. But this doesn't happen only with visits to your life coach. If you are doing the work, then your visits will become fewer and farther between while you are advancing yourself on your own. If you choose not to do the homework, then it will take much longer to advance, and it will mean many more visits to the life coach for quite some time. You may ask, "what am I supposed to be doing at home?" What I can honestly say is that you have to build your own energy and psychic abilities. And this is what I do and love to do. Utilize my abilities to help others heal from traumas, develop their psychic abilities and not only change their world by changing their life but help others realize by doing so they are also doing their part in changing the world. This is what I do as a psychic medium, life coach, teacher, and energy healer.

CHAPTER TEN

UNDERSTANDING HOW TO DEVELOP YOUR OWN PSYCHIC ABILITIES.

Now the work begins! Time to accept and understand the fact that every one of us has psychic abilities and that is just a fact. You are human. You have the capability of developing each psychic ability listed throughout this book. Have I mastered them all? No, but I know that it is possible. I also know it is not easy, as I continue to develop my own abilities. My abilities continue to change the more I use them and with the energy work I do. This leaves me open to the possibility that I could have abilities in five years that I do not have now.

The Earth is changing, and as she does so, the changing energies are awakening the psychic abilities in all of us. Many people who were born with this high vibratory gene I spoke of earlier have not been using it or have been suppressing it and will have no choice but to start using it as more experiences begin to happen to them. And those not born with such a gene may begin to experience things they had no idea were possible for them. The best advice I have is to absolutely STOP doubting yourself! When you think you saw something out of the corner of your eye, you did! When you go to a house and don't like the way it feels, trust me, there is a reason and you are correct! If you think someone is watching you, yet nobody is there, you are right! If you hear ringing in your ears, or you think someone whispered your name behind your back. They are communicating! Time to wake up and start listening!

Start paying attention to the signs. They are giving you signs, and every sign means something. Have you been finding feathers a lot lately? Those are gifts from the Angels. Have you had an unusual encounter with an animal or bug? Once I had a bee circle me eight times, just flying circles around me to get my attention. Or, perhaps, an unusual amount, of butterflies were dancing around you? One time at the park, my grandson had dozens of them fluttering around him and dancing with him. This was so noticeable, there was no writing it off as just butterflies of the season flying around. I have never witnessed anything like it in my life. One time I couldn't help but notice that for several weeks I had hawks following me. I would walk outside, and three hawks were there to follow me on my walk. I would drive somewhere, and three hawks followed and swooped around my car, it was impossible not to notice them trying to get my attention. What does it mean when these signs are being given to us? These are all signs from our Angels, guides or loved ones from the Other Side, and it is easy enough to look up their meaning on the Internet. I have a hard time myself remembering the individual meaning of each one, so I often look up the meaning of Native American animal totems and then add in whatever animal it is that had made their appearance. I find the answers to be very accurate and resonate quite well with whatever is going on with me at the time. I usually look up three sites to see the results, and I often find them to match up with each other. You also may ask your guides and Angels to help you by giving you a sign, or even your animal totems.

Another way to connect with your guides, is in your dreams. You see, while we are dreaming, we all are wide open to receive information and can communicate much easier with our support team on the other side. Not only is it easier to communicate, but we also bring back knowledge from them as well. Just tell them before you go to sleep, or basically anytime you wish, because they don't deal in time. Everything is now. Just inform them that you would like to receive messages in your dreams and be sure to keep your book next to your bed and write down anything you get, no matter how small.

The absolute best way to get in touch with your guides and Angels, inner and higher self, is to meditate. You must learn how to meditate. This is the most important thing you will do when it comes to advancing yourself and connecting with your guides. Besides, just one hour a day of quieting the mind has been proven to help with IQ levels, increased focus and memory, reducing any number of medical issues, including stress. This is vital for spiritual advancement. Through your meditation you will slowly but surely begin to open your mind up to start seeing things, as well as hearing, and knowing things. These are very significant, even though they may seem so slight at the time. How do you meditate? There are, mindfulness, or beginner meditation classes that you can do or meditation circles to join. I offer different types of meditation at my center. Energy healers often teach or know who can teach you meditation or are aware of local meditation groups. There are many groups out there to get together with, or perhaps just learn on your own. I personally bought a book about chakras and meditation in 2000 and taught myself how to meditate. I had no intention of doing so, but it was kind of hard not to buy the book. My guide practically pushed it in my face when I was at the bookstore just browsing. Guided meditations may also be found quite easily online. Assistance in meditation is out there and only requires some searching on your part, but they can easily be found. Gaia T.V. is a great resource as well. They have wonderful shows on many things, including information on and understanding meditation.

I continuously keep bringing this up, but the importance of T'ai-chi or Qigong is not to be underestimated. This is energy exercise and it helps develop your connections to the energy of the universe. This energy of the universe, of which we are all a part of, is truly our connection to our psychic selves. In China they have many psychics within their population, and they will often attest to the fact that it's their daily Qigong practice that does this. In fact, the entire country is so into their Qigong that the parks fill up with residents at 4:00 p.m. to participate in their daily Qigong ritual. This is a practice in becoming the energy, remember, we are all energy and what is psychic abilities? Energy! Tapping into energy that is what you are doing regardless of what ability you are using! We have T'ai-chi masters in the Far East who are so advanced that they can create fire from thin air. Wow. Pyrokinesis at its best right? They also can levitate and move objects just like the Jedi knights. Hmm, telekinetic abilities, too, from T'ai-chi? Apparently. My son often moves small objects, or knocks over dollar bills with his energy using Chi. So yes, it is possible with much training to do so.

It is important to also include yoga into your meditation and energy workouts. Yoga does work differently yet coincides with the other things I have mentioned. Yoga incorporates the breath, and while so does T'ai-chi it is different. Yoga teaches the connection between the mind, body and spirit. The breath is your connection with the spirit self, which ultimately helps you to connect to your higher self. First, you must learn to connect with the inner self and understand this inner self before you learn to understand your higher self, and what the higher self has to offer you. Oftentimes, when I am doing automatic writing, it is my higher self, doing it.

Next, it is vital to learn about and understand your chakras. There are hundreds of chakras and this can be quite overwhelming in the beginning, I suggest you do what most of us do and learn about the main seven chakras first. These are energy vortexes in the body that absolutely help you to connect with your higher and inner self, as well as assist in keeping your energies balanced. This results in emotional balancing, level-headedness, focus and a rise in overall energy levels.

Another important point for developing your abilities is to eat healthy foods. Some might wonder what the difference is, in my psychic abilities if I eat junk food, or meat, but the truth is a lot. Sugar is very damaging, and not sugar from fruit or raw honey from a local honey farm. I mean processed sugars and it can be brown sugar, white sugar, powdered sugar, syrup-you name it. Even raw organic sugar is bad, which is what I switched to in my process of weaning off the sugars, and artificial is the worst. Start in stages, if you must, but start putting in the effort towards getting rid of the sugar, as well as gluten. A very close friend of mine had realized, after a few of her friends went on a no gluten diet, that she can see their energies change colors and expand! Again, begin to reduce it at first, if you must, but begin the process of getting rid of it. Then we have meat. My entire life I have struggled to eat meat and it often gave me a weird sickness in my stomach that I could not explain. Often, I would be eating a turkey sandwich and feel sick, then peel the turkey out and continue eating with no problems. Then a few years ago the only meats I usually could eat began to make me feel sick too. I read an article about how it is quite common for empaths to have issues eating meat because they psychically connect to the animals they are eating, particularly if they had a difficult death in the process. This made perfect sense to me and I have since given up meat. However, we shouldn't give up meat just for empathic reasons. These animals are our cousins and they have souls just like ours. Perhaps you have been a cow in a past life, or you will be one in the next life. I have taken people into past lives who say they were animals such as a cat, and my horse claims to be a relation to Ernest Hemingway in a past life.

But, even beyond that, meat it is a low vibratory food. When you are doing all this energy work to raise your vibrations, then lower them with low vibratory foods, you are contradicting the work you are doing. So, what are high vibratory foods? Food that is raised in the ground with the suns, energy, such as fruits and vegetables that are chemical free. We are not meant to eat those awful poisons they spray on our foods. Nuts are good, as is local raw honey where the bees are treated right, local farm fresh eggs are good. I have had chickens myself and I can assure you that the chicken can lay eggs without a rooster present. Not only can she, but she will no matter what. And if you do not collect them, they will rot. Even if you do have a rooster, the eggs will not begin to develop until the hen decides to sit.

It has been scientifically proven that cells, even from vegetables, fruit, nuts, and farm eggs do react to being cooked and eaten. If you talk to your food and it doesn't have to be out loud, just explain that you are going to eat them, and you are grateful for their contribution to your health and livelihood, this will raise their vibrations, reducing trauma from consumption. If you raise your own food, then be sure to talk to the plants and tell them you love them and appreciate them. Thank them when you harvest, and you will have a high-vibratory food source that will absolutely change your vibrations. How does this make me more psychic? When you are traveling at a high vibratory pattern, it is easier for you to connect with your guides, as well as making it easier for them to connect with you. Remember they are traveling at an extremely high vibration and we are at a very low vibration, so anything we can do to increase our vibrations is a step towards becoming more psychic.

Another important thing that you must do to increase, or at the very least reduce the decreasing or your vibration, is zero alcohol. Alcohol is a low vibratory substance. Think about it, if you take a class educating you on drugs and alcohol, they will tell you that alcohol is a downer and not an upper like some other substances that alter your current vibratory pattern, such as marijuana. I hardly ever drink but a glass of wine or a mixed drink on occasion. This was okay for me until my guides informed me, I was to drink zero alcohol. I said that will be easy to give up my one or two glasses a year. I was at the health food store and there was a lady offering wine samples. I tasted it and thought, "Wow, I really like this one, so perhaps I will go ahead and buy a bottle." I took the bottle home and a few days later decided to have a glass late one night after everyone went to bed. I settled in to enjoy a glass of wine and watch some Cosmic Disclosure on Gaia, when the most horrible taste entered my mouth. It was like bad vinegar. What was that? I tasted it again and thought, "Wow, this doesn't taste anything like the sample." Then I heard my guide say, "No alcohol means zero alcohol." Yep, they did that, they made it taste so horrible I threw out the rest of the bottle and learned my lesson on drinking. When they say no meat then no meat, or you will get sick. When they say no alcohol, then no alcohol or you will get sick. Now my guides are telling me to give up dairy. I have been reducing it quite consistently and, luckily, they have not made me sick yet. I'm down to a couple times a month, but I must admit that Haagan Daz ice cream is a weakness of mine. That seems to be my only hang-up with the sugar and dairy, for the time being.

Some substances, like marijuana, will get you high for a reason. It raises your vibration and can assist you in your efforts of raising your vibration and connecting with your guides. I currently don't use it because it has zero effect on me. I vibrate too high for it. I know people who do, and it can help elevate the energy work that you do. I would like to caution that it may assist but should not be used as a crutch to avoid the real work that has to be done. It is not for daily use and intensions should be set beforehand. What would you like to learn or accomplish?

Another way to increase your psychic abilities is through wearing jewelry. One night when I was connected, a friend's guide spoke to me at great length on the importance of earrings. It was a 45-minute rant, so I will share just the highlights here and spare you the lengthy lecture we all received. First, we should all be wearing earrings, but there are stipulations as to what kind of earrings. They absolutely must be real gold, either white or yellow, or real silver. These metals are conductors of energy, and if you don't think so then investigate what powers your electronics. Cheap metals will inhibit this energy from flowing, so it is better not to wear the fake stuff. Next, never ever wear anything that resembles a shield, which includes the cross, an X, the peace sign, or whatever. If it resembles a shield, then it will act like one and it blocks out your guides from talking to you. Gems are very good to wear, but the intention must be right. Example: If you are wearing two-carrot diamonds, just to show off that you can afford two carrot diamonds they will never work well for you. Your energies will never balance right. Excellent ones to wear are things like amethyst or lapis lazuli, if communication is what you seek, however, if you get a feeling or a knowing to wear something else then do it. This is your psychic connection to the gems, and they are calling you because they know they will work well with your energy field. Necklaces are basically the same rule, but instead of blocking your hearing they can block your Heart and Throat chakras. So, follow the same rules. There are some wonderful symbols out there that can enhance your psychic and spiritual advancement, if you are wearing a necklace like a trifecta because other people are, and it just looks cool but you have no idea what it is, or what it does or why you are wearing it, then it won't really work for you, and possibly could work against you if you are not experienced with such symbols. So, as a rule of thumb, buy powerful symbols you are familiar with unless you feel it calling you, then do your research and learn about what it is. Rings and bracelets and anklets are to follow the same rules but have less significance in the way of blocking your psychic connections. The earrings are the guides biggest complaint, because then people cannot hear them.

The most important thing when developing your psychic abilities is to keep your integrity, no matter what. If you don't know something, then say you don't know. Or if you don't understand what information is coming through, don't try too hard to come up with it because it always reveals itself in time, just say this is what I got, and I don't understand the meaning. But, if this is really what you see, hear or feel then don't second-guess yourself, even if someone says it doesn't make sense. Stick to the information you received. Do not try to get information they want you to get, but only what comes through. Believe me I know it can be disappointing when someone doesn't get the answers they are looking for; it doesn't mean they didn't get the answers they were supposed to have. We do not fit into the box, that has been predetermined of what is psychic and under no circumstances should you falter on your integrity to fit into that box or try to make people happy by telling them what they expect. The best thing is to tell people to never have any expectations going into a reading because it never will work in the way they expected it to work. Know that going into it and do not falter in your integrity no matter what someone else says, thinks, or feels about the information coming through.

Absolutely know to the core of your being, that we all have the same equal value and worth as any other entity, in all of creation! You are subservient to none, and none are subservient to you! Know your power and self-worth for it is extraordinary! We are all one, who have come from the same one infinite creator, and there are no special people given a special gift that the others are not good enough, or loved enough, to get. Also, it is no accident that some people can access their psychic abilities, and some must work much harder at it. You were 100% involved in the decision making and planning of this lifetime, and that includes the good with the bad. Some are not more famous or powerful or richer than you are for no reason. You personally could have chosen that path as well as they did, however, you have decided that this is your path, and you have a very good reason to experience what you have chosen to experience.

And, lastly, remember to always open your connections with love because only through love do we access our true intuitive selves and communicate with our most authentic self. Not the self that was told to you, but the authentic self that is connected to source, the guides, the Angels, animal totems, and mostly, to the infinite creator that created us through the greatest power of all; which is true, honest, and unconditional love. Thus, we are all one!

REFERENCES

DR. BRUCE GOLDBERG- MASTERS DEGREE IN PSYCHOLOGY, HYPNOTHERAPIST, PAST LIFE REGRESSIONIST AND AUTHOR

DELORIS CANNON-HYPNOTHERAPIST, PAST LIFE REGRESSIONIST AND NEW YORK TIMES BEST SELLING AUTHOR

NANCY ANN TAPPE- TEACHER, COUNSELOR AND AUTHOR

LEE CARROLL AND JAN TOBER-CHANNELERS, PSYCHICS AND BEST SELLING AUTHORS

BARBERA MARCINIAK-CHANNELER AND AUTHOR

EMPOWERING YOUR INDIGO CHILD BY WAYNE DOSICK AND ELLEN KAUFMAN DOSICK

MEG BLACKBURN LOSEY-ARCHEOLOGIST, ANTHROPOLOGIST, AUTHOR, MASTER HEALER AND MEDICAL INTUITIVE AND RADIO SHOW HOST

CHINA'S SUPER PSYCHICS BY PAUL DONG AND THOMAS RAFFILL

SYLVIA BROWNE AUTHOR AND PSYCHIC

THE LAW OF ONE BY CARLA RUECKERT, DON ELKINS AND JAMES MCCARTHY

JOURNAL OF A STAR SEED BY CHARIS BROWN MALLOY

HISTORY CHANNEL'S ANCIENT ALIENS AND HANGER ONE

LINDA MOULTON HOWE, AUTHOR, REPORTER, RESEARCHER AND HOST.

DR STEPHEN GREER- THE DISCLOSURE PROJECT, UFOLOGIST, TRAUMATOLOGIST, MOVIE PRODUCER

CHRISTOPHER O'BRIAN AUTHOR THE MYSTERIOUS VALLEY, ENTER THE VALLEY, SECRETS OF THE MYSTERIOUS VALLEY AND STALKING THE HERD.

RICHARD DOLAN-AUTHOR, HISTORIAN AND PUBLISHER

DAVID WILCOCK-LECTURER, FILMMAKER, RESEARCHER, AND NEW YORK TIME BESTSELLING AUTHOR

George Noorey- radio and T.V. talk show host

Corey Goode-producer, insider informant and guest speaker for radio and talk shows

Emery Smith-United States Air Force retired, scientist, and insider whistleblower, TV and radio show guest speaker

Pjotr Garjajev-biophysicist and molecular biologist

Luke Chan-author

Chi Lel-Dr Pang Ming-energy healer

Nikola Tesla-inventor, mechanical engineer, and electrical engineer

Dr. Masaru Emoto-pseudoscientist and author

Zdzislaw Beksinski- painter, sculptor and photographer

Rose Inserra- author, speaker and dream interpreter

Robert Simmons- founder and sponsor of the crystal conference, heaven and earth crystal shop and author

Coast to Coast AM radio

Gaia T.V.

truebetteryou.com

Emoto

spiritualityandhealth.com

Dr. Laura the intuition physician YouTube

artclesmercola.com

www.wowzone.com

wakeupworld.com

The Dream Dictionary by Rose Inserra

Lightning Source UK Ltd.
Milton Keynes UK
UKHW042016060820
367821UK00001B/23